M000043303

ENDORSEMENTS

The authors seamlessly meld the fields of employment, economics, politics and government policies into a make sense career management system. Their insights may well have you thinking "How did they know that about my career and jobsearch?"

— **BOB SCARPETTA,** CMC, CRMS.
TAMPA/ST. PETERSBURG, FLORIDA

* * *

Careermageddon's unique selling point is its synthesis of macro-economics with the business of finding a career pathway in a VUCA (volatile, uncertain, complex and ambiguous) world. In a world where jobs for life no longer exist, the smart person scans the environment for opportunities and is creative about seizing those opportunities.

— **PETER COOK,** MD *HUMAN DYNAMICS AND THE ACADEMY OF ROCK. ROCHESTER, UK*

* * *

Reading the book I come to the staggering conclusion that the best economists are not sitting in central London but in Cardiff in Wales! The insight of the global economy, trades, banks and so called recession is a fascinating story made quite easy to read and understand. The book progresses then into the labyrinth of career management which is a complicated minefield by itself. I guess we are all in one or another way involved in careers, recruitment, selection processes and can relate to the subjects in many ways. Neil is a gifted writer and the world is waiting for his publications.

— *AXEL KOSTER,* GENERAL MANAGER,
THE MANHATTAN GROUP. MELBOURNE, AUSTRALIA

* * *

Careermagedon is not the average quick fix, self-help, self-improvement paperback we find at airports and train stations around the western world. It's more like an action-packed blockbuster thriller for those that want to understand their working life better. *Careermagedon* is the long read that we should all pick up from time to time for a "big picture" understanding of the global work place. It explains in easy to follow narrative, full of useful examples and cases, how our own very localised world is being shaped by technology, innovation, competition and change. On my own reading of *Careermagedon* it wasn't just that I came to recognise the mistakes I have made in failing to nurture my working life. *Careermagedon* provides the explanations, a structure and processes for setting that right. In the context of today's connected and competitive work landscape career change now seems less daunting and depressing, more exciting and appealing. Expect to be enlightened!

— *JOHN HANNA,* MANAGING DIRECTOR,
GDP GLOBAL DEVELOPMENT, LONDON.

* * *

Careermageddon is an astute analysis of the global jobs crisis and its impact on how people manage their career progression. If you've been frustrated in your quest for the job that's right for you, this book will help you sort out your fantasies from reality. It could help you trim your campaign by weeks or even months.

Understanding what is actually going on in the economy and in the hiring processes at your target companies will support you in making wise decisions both in the short term and throughout your career path.

* * *

Our work environment has changed dramatically. Marcia LaReau and Neil Patrick explain how and why with remarkable insight. You must have a career strategy to keep on earning. And not your parents' career strategy. These career experts show you how to develop the strategy that fits your needs. We all need help with our careers. Your help is in this book. A great career guide.

* * *

"The only certainty in life is change." This book talks about financial changes in our economy, the government's response, and the resulting global financial crisis, but puts the onus to do so on the individual reader. The authors do a terrific job in guiding the reader to understand the need to be engaged in and take charge of one's career development, and thus one's financial future, putting into perspective why proactively managing both is a necessity.

The first part of the book discusses the origins of the Global Jobs Crisis and the Great Recession of 2008. The surprising main culprit? The world's addiction to credit. As much as possible, the authors have put the origins of our current economic climate into layman's terms, citing examples and case studies.

The second part of the book is where the individual takes action. While "passion" is important, the authors stress that only following passions will lead to an uncertain and most likely gloomy financial future. The sound advice from this book will lead readers to not only plan a couple years ahead, but use the strategies to map out a secure financial future while doing work they enjoy.

— *EDYTHE RICHARDS, CAREER COUNSELOR AND FOUNDER, A TOP CAREER, SERVING THE WASHINGTON, DC METRO AND BEYOND.*

* * *

Marcia LaRéau and Neil Patrick have nailed it in *Careermageddon*. Careers and Career Management have changed forever. Marcia and Neil give the reader an in-depth explanation why it has changed (yes, we need to know why) and then give the reader the 21st century strategies to use in moving their careers forward.
Bravo to Marcia and Neil.

— *MARC MILLER, PRESIDENT CAREER PIVOT. AUSTIN, TX USA*

* * *

"I really enjoyed reading *Careermageddon*, which I found to be a very entertaining and intelligent book. The authors provide several eye-opening insights as to why the world finds itself trapped in a huge economic mess and why technological progress has resulted in job destruction rather than creation. If you want some practical advice on how to succeed as a careerist in this radically altered economic landscape you need to buy this book NOW.

— *GEORGE VERDOLAGA, AMAZON BEST-SELLING AUTHOR OF 'THE MAVERICK EFFECT' AND 'THE GAME CHANGER', VANCOUVER, BRITISH COLUMBIA, CANADA*

* * *

Careermageddon explores the reason why today's workforce is suffering and how to make the best of the changing landscape.

I was intrigued by the authors' explanation of how the recession came about, particularly how the worlds' banks placed workers in financial and emotional debt by carelessly and unwisely lending money. The result, as we know, was a global economic bust that forced many people out of jobs. Jobs that were supposed to be secure.

This book will be of great value to people attempting to understand why the workforce became a shambles and, more importantly, what to do about it.

— BOB MCINTOSH, *CAREER AND LINKEDIN STRATEGIST, LOWELL, MASSACHUSETTS, USA.*

* * *

Marcia LaReau and Neil Patrick have written a critical book outlining the future of work and the twin necessities to 1) take charge of your own destiny, and 2) to continually be flexible. No longer can people rely on others to plan, cultivate, and develop them in a projected and foreseeable career path. Instead, people must proactively take the reins to guide themselves. In the old days, mariners would seek out maps to guide them; often, on these maps would be "Here there be dragons . . ." Marcia and Neil don't just mark these areas, they identify the dragons.

— DAVID HUNT, PE, *MECHANICAL ENGINEER, JOBSEARCH HELPER AND NETWORKER, EMPLOYMENT PRACTICES GADFLY, AND UNCOMFORTABLE THOUGHT-PROCESS IGNITER. GREATER BOSTON AREA*

* * *

This work will be a boon to many who seek to both understand their place in our multi-faceted local, national, and global economies, as well as to navigate their place in those ever-changing tides.

— THOMAS MORIARTY PMP, CSM, *PROJECT MANAGEMENT PROFESSIONAL. SEATTLE, WASHINGTON*

* * *

Steady employment, satisfying work, a secure future . . . this book shows that it is possible in this new ever-changing world.

Readable, understandable, and encouraging, "Careermageddon" first answers the question, "Why?" Why has the world changed, why has the economy changed, why has the job market changed? With the understanding of "Why," how do we plan in an uncertain world?

"Careermageddon" is a practical guide to envisioning and walking new career paths in the 21st century. It equips the reader with tools to evaluate current and potential jobs. Action items guide the reader to a more efficient and effective method of conducting a jobsearch in the current climate.

This book is like a pair of binoculars that reveals the future with greater clarity; equipping the reader to tweak today and prepare for tomorrow.

I heartily endorse this book for people searching to discover ways to find satisfying work for a fulfilling life at every stage of their career.

— *Amy Riebs Mills, Classical music composer and conductor. Washington D.C. Metro Area*

* * *

Marcia and Neil have written a book that is current, relatable and amazingly insightful. They have taken complex economic policy and presented it in clear, understandable terms through realistic and relevant case studies and language, while relating it to the process of designing a career plan that is satisfying, sustainable and financially manageable.

Reading this book will make you aware of the dire importance of the need for an ongoing career progression plan and the thinking that is needed to successfully plan, track and manage your career in today's ever changing technological environment. This book puts you on a path for finding and maintaining a satisfying and rewarding career no matter what stage of life you are in.

— DON MARINO, PROGRAM MANAGER, COASTAL COUNTIES WORKFORCE, INC., SOUTHERN MAINE COMMUNITY COLLEGE. BRUNSWICK, MAINE

* * *

Marcia and Neil have tackled the "Macro" world of work in the global economy and the systemic elements of economic fragility. This context sets up the core principle that each person must control their own career, navigating economic winds independently. To help each worker do so, they provide detailed steps for getting real and getting serious about designing a career that delivers the components necessary to call it a success. If you want to reflect deeply on your world and your career, this is a great place to start.

— REED MACMILLAN, FOUNDER OF VIBRAINT LLC, (PROVIDING CONSULTING THAT HELPS COMPANIES THRIVE SMARTLY). HARTFORD, CONNECTICUT AREA

Careermageddon

CRACKING THE 21ST CENTURY CAREER CODE

Marcia LaReau | Neil Patrick

Forward Motion, LLC

Forward Motion, LLC
P.O. Box 855
Bloomfield, CT 06002

978-0-9992062-0-1 Print
978-0-9992062-1-8 eBook

Dedication

*This book is dedicated to everyone
who wonders if we are writing about them. We are.*

CONTENTS

FOREWORD
by Mark S. Babbitt

Careers are crazy things. Just when you think you have it all figured out, something—or someone—comes along and blows everything up.

You may have picked up this book because you're among the many who have been unemployed for what seems like forever. Maybe you've just lost your last job. Or perhaps you're trying to land your first job. Regardless, your career isn't going exactly as you imagined—or dreamed. Frustration has set in. You're worried about not just the future, but the present. You're just not sure how to compete in the Social Age jobsearch. You may even feel like you're fighting a duel, but the other guy keeps shooting on '1' while you're counting to '3'.

And then along comes a resource that helps put everything into perspective. Along comes, *Careermageddon*.

And you not only start to understand your professional life better, you learn how the global economy works. You gain an understanding that—despite all the bad news—every day, people get hired for their skills, passion and grit. You come to know that some people—with the same background, education and experience as you—make it work. They found work. *They are happy.*

And you want to be one of them.

But to do that, you must learn how you fit into this new economic engine. You must know your role. Well past what would be considered job requirements and your basic qualifications, you must understand your raw potential—and unique value—better than you ever have before.

And you will. Because in your hands you now have a career survival guide that will help you thrive in any economic downturn; in any crisis.

In *Careermageddon: Cracking the 21st Century Career Code,* authors Marcia LaReau and Neil Patrick have created a contemporary career guide no job seeker should be without. It's a manual that not only provides proven and practical career advice, but also keen insight into how our current reality—and economy—works.

That is what separates this book from others you've read. The authors go well past what you might expect from a typical career book to help you understand today's global job market. They help you unlearn what you thought you knew about finding work. Then, so you can play the game at a master level, they've broken down all the rules in an easy to understand way full of "ah-ha" moments.

After all, if you don't know the rules . . . how can you win the game?

And those rules? They are always changing. This inherent instability is a curse if we don't know how to respond. It can be a blessing if we do. If we can see ahead of the curve, we don't mind that another one is coming. We start to take those curves faster, with more confidence. And soon, we start to see the volatile, ambiguous world of work as a place we can call home. Instead of a scary place where career dreams go to die, this strange land called the "Gig Economy" becomes a gold mine of opportunity.

Marcia and Neil are the perfect guides for this land of opportunity—and your new adventure. Leveraging years of experience in the career space, they provide more than just how to get hired. They help you understand how work works in the 21st century.

After reading *Careermageddon,* you'll understand which skills are in chronic shortage—and which skills no longer make you special in the eyes of an employer. You'll know how to develop and market the skills that help make you infinitely employable even in an ultra-competitive job market. Before you get to the last page, you'll have the cornerstones necessary to build both a strategic and practical personal response to whatever comes around the next curve.

So read on. Learn how to embrace the new world of work; the one that is always changing and forever unpredictable. Understand the current pain of employers. Then build a career strategy that will ease that pain—one that clearly presents you as the solution to employers' problems, now and in the future.

And along the way, learn how to clearly articulate your skills, values and personal culture in a way that distances you from everyone else.

Your career—along with meaningful work and a fulfilling life—starts here. On page one.

What are you waiting for? Turn the page!

Mark S. Babbitt
Leadership and Career Mentor, Blogger, Speaker and Author
Twitter: @MarkSBabbitt

PREFACE

Paula Bray is 53 years old. She grew up in the San Francisco Bay Area, later moving to Tacoma during junior high school.

She earned a master's degree in 2007 and was later accepted into a doctoral program at Georgia Southern University. She took a few classes while enrolled in the program before returning to Bakersfield to take up a position at the local college.

Since losing her job, she has been forced to live in an RV while scratching a tiny monthly income from part-time work (The Economic Collapse Blog, n.d.).

Bray's story is fairly typical. She is a middle-class person, educated, intelligent, and hardworking. But this didn't prevent her from joining the ranks of the long-term unemployed. In March 2014, in desperation, she wrote this letter to Barack Obama (Bray, 2014):

> Dear Mr. President,
>
> I write to you today because I have nowhere else to turn. I lost my full-time job in September

2012. I have only been able to find part-time employment—16 hours each week at $12 per hour—but I don't work that every week. For the month of December, my net pay was $365. My husband and I now live in an RV at a campground because of my job loss. Our monthly rent is $455 and that doesn't include utilities. We were given this 27-ft. 1983 RV when I lost my job.

This is America today. We have no running water; we use a hose to fill jugs. We have no shower but the campground does. We have a toilet but it only works when the sewer line doesn't freeze—if it freezes, we use the campground's restrooms. At night, in my bed, when it's cold out, my blanket can freeze to the wall of the RV. We don't have a stove or an oven, just a microwave, so regular-food cooking is out. Recently we found a small toaster oven on sale so we can bake a little now because eating only microwaved food just wasn't working for us. We don't have a refrigerator, just an icebox (a block of ice cost about $1.89). It keeps things relatively cold. If it's freezing outside, we just put things on the picnic table.

Unfortunately, we can't buy things in bulk because they will go bad before we can use them. We can't buy dry goods in bulk either, because there is no room to store them anywhere in the RV.

We are very lucky that the campground has showers, but it costs 25 cents for two minutes. There have been times when we couldn't afford a shower and had to resort to bathing in the campground restroom sink. There was a shower in the RV but the plumbing has deteriorated so now we use it as a closet.

The walls of the RV are not well insulated, so many times the inside gets wet from condensation. That means all of the blankets that we have stored above the bed may end up moldy if we don't remove them [and] dry them periodically. There is mold under the carpet on the floor and there is mold along the walls behind our seats. But we keep it clean the best we can. The heating system in the RV no longer functions, so we have a small radiator-type floor heater and we move it around to dry the floor to keep it from molding.

My husband is bipolar and was considered disabled and was receiving SSI. Prior to my job loss, he was seen for 12 minutes by a disability physician, never asked about his [bipolar] condition and was kicked off disability. He had received $1,000 per month, but it is gone.

After I lost my job at a college, we moved from Kern County in California, where the unemployment rate is over 10 percent, to the Pacific Northwest where the unemployment rate is lower to be near my son and grandson but without gas money, we still can't visit them.

So now we sit. I apply for so many jobs daily. I have a Master's degree and have been in the workforce for over 30 years. Why can't I find a job? I have marketable skills. My credit is gone (credit score of 570) and so I am no longer being considered for jobs in the "real" world. I am only ever considered for government jobs and even then, they usually know who they plan to hire but they have to go through the process. So here we sit.

I had been receiving unemployment benefits from California but now that the unemployment rate for the state is lower, there are no more funds coming in.

My husband can't find a job. No one wants to hire me. Luckily, the State of Washington has decided to provide us with $300 in food stamps each month but it still isn't enough to survive on. All of our savings is gone. I no longer have any retirement savings. Nothing.

By the end of this month, we will be without anywhere to turn.

Your devoted constituent,
Paula Bray

She tries to make the most of her situation as she battles with unemployment. The most tragic and important thing about Paula Bray's situation is that it is far from unique.

Yet despite the desperate situation she has encountered since losing her job, Bray says that she considers herself fortunate. "I don't want pity," she says. "I want a job."

This is the harsh reality of modern America for the middle classes. Unemployment and destitution are only ever a breath away for millions of smart, educated, and hardworking people. And yet employers report they cannot get the skilled workers they seek.

What on earth is going on? And what can you do to ensure you don't become the next victim of the global jobs crisis?

The answer is that you can do plenty. And that's why we wrote this book.

Marcia LaReau in Connecticut, USA
Neil Patrick in Cardiff, Wales, UK

ACKNOWLEDGEMENTS

This book would not have been possible without the assistance of many exceptional people who have helped, inspired, informed and encouraged us over this two-year project.

Firstly, we should thank Mark Babbitt, who was kind enough to write the foreword. Mark's quite brilliant book written with Ted Coiné, *A World Gone Social,* is essential reading for anyone interested in how the digital world has changed our world especially in relation to business and jobs.

Jorg Stegemann of Kennedy Executive served us most generously as our inside contact into the world of recruitment. Likewise, the most high-profile recruiter on social media, Axel Koster of the Manhattan Group encouraged us and was generous with his insights. Recruiters have really hectic lives, so we are especially grateful to these two gentlemen.

Jeremy Rifkin's groundbreaking work including *The Third Industrial Revolution* and *The Zero Marginal Cost Society* provided us with immense insights into the enormous global transformations which are reshaping our world.

Ken Gronbach's books on, *The Age Curve* and *Decades of Differences,* on demographics was exceptionally helpful to us in understanding this aspect of the evolving workforce.

Jesse Colombo's analyses of global markets and bubbles provided valuable insights into the financial forces which are impacting jobs.

We must also thank the people who read and commented on our draft script and were so generous with their praise: John Hanna, Bob MacIntosh, John Tarnoff, Edythe Richards, George Verdolaga, Axel Koster, John Eldridge, Marc Miller, Bob Scarpetta, Peter Cook, Amy R. Mills, Don Marino, Robin Bienemann, Judith Rosenthal, David Hunt, and Diana Schneidman.

Our editor, Paul Hawley did a sterling job of turning our prose into a much more polished and readable piece of work. Boris Margolin took our ideas and turned them into images which expressed things visually much better than we could do in words. He also brought our ideas to life for the cover design.

Last but not least, the small army of people on social media and in everyday life, who have helped and inspired us on the journey especially; Susan Joyce, Patricia Frame, Kim Marino, Phyllis Mufson, Stacy Donovan Zapar, Julie Bishop, David Nicola, John Siracusa, Ibro Palic, Yittah Lawrence, Andrew Ginsburg, Ernest Heybud, Tony Restell, Mary Eileen Williams, Abby Kohut, Buzz Brindle, Marc Miller,

ACKNOWLEDGEMENTS

Bob Carlson, Jeff Grant, Jennifer Bulman, Trish Thomas, Janet Nelson, Jonathan Whitcraft, Angelene Croasdale, Jackie Peterson, Elaine Grimm, Dean and Shirley Wilson, Alicia M. J-Warren, Michael Allen, and Reed MacMillan.

INTRODUCTION

"The primary will of the world is no longer about peace or freedom or even democracy; it is not about having a family, and it is neither about God nor about owning a home or land. The will of the world is first and foremost to have a good job."

— JIM CLIFTON: THE COMING JOBS WAR, 2011

We're all tired of crises. There's the climate change crisis. There's an energy and housing crisis. There's a global terror crisis. And we've still not recovered from the 2008 financial crisis. (Don't relax just yet—we're due another one of these soon.)

And yet the crisis which gets almost no attention is the global jobs crisis. Which is odd if we feel any affinity with the words of Jim Clifton (CEO of Gallup) above, quoted from his book, *The Coming Jobs War*. It's the absence of this information (and ignorance about what to do with it) that prompted us to write this book.

Six important points

There are six points we want to make clear before you begin this book.

1. We know that people need income to survive. And they need good and steady income throughout their entire adult lives if they are going to prosper. This is getting ever harder to attain due to the global economic situation and the rise of technology.

2. Governments and institutions recognize this situation and may try to help. However, there is no precedent or policy that can quickly and reliably alter the course of the coming economic changes.

3. We believe that the only way to approach the current situation and these coming changes is for individuals to protect themselves and their families by increasing their employability and attractiveness to employers.

4. We expect to earn our revenue stream. We see this as a life skill that is just as important as any professional qualification. It has been made clear to us that hard work alone is not going to create the revenue we need. Therefore, we have to understand the market and apply our work ethic in the right place!

5. We wrote this book as a guide to help you understand the changes in the jobs market, and how to manage your skills and knowledge to survive the global jobs crisis.

6. We believe that everyone will have to become their own "personal economist." To do this effectively, it will require an understanding of the principles presented in Part One of this book.

What this book does and doesn't do

This book doesn't preach about how businesses should act toward their employees. It doesn't advocate entrepreneurship or the free market or education or any other panacea. It doesn't argue for or against government policies. In that sense, it is politically neutral—although it will probably still irritate some people from all sides of the political spectrum.

This book is not about how we design a fairer, more just society. It's about how ordinary people can continue to survive in an era when technology, globalization, offshoring, and the transition to a digital economy are killing jobs off faster than the world can create new ones.

This book isn't for policymakers, economists, or employers. It's for everyday people who depend on their ability to earn a living to survive. It's for people who are too busy to spend time figuring out what's really going on. And it's for people who would rather respond to these calamities by planning their future, going to work, and knowing how to think about it and manage the situation to ensure that they can earn a good living.

This book adopts the premise that the world is the way it is, and what will determine our own individual success or failure is how we interact with it. This attitude is not new. What is new is that the pace of change is accelerating so fast that people and employers, let alone our governments and institutions, can no longer keep up. Consequently, we all need a strategy to cope, survive, and enjoy our lives without constant worry about uncontrollable change.

This book is simply about how everyday men and women in the developed Western economies need to reevaluate how they think about their jobs and their careers in the future. If you are currently without a job and want one, that future is right now. If you currently have a job, then right now you need to think about what you will do when you no longer have it.

The global jobs crisis is real—we didn't make this up

The global jobs crisis is real. In fact, in 2014, two years after one of your authors, Neil, used the term in the subtitle of his blog, none other than the World Bank issued a report that described the global jobs crisis in forensic detail.

The World Bank Report went more or less unremarked upon by the mainstream media. It was titled in typical government speak and somewhat benignly "G-20 labor markets: outlook, key challenges and policy responses" (G20 Labour and Employment Ministerial Meeting [LEMM], 2014). Behind this dull bureaucratic title lay the starkest confirmation we'd seen, which described in depressing detail the true nature of the global jobs problem.

The report stated: "The world is facing a global jobs crisis that is killing the chances of reigniting economic growth." But worse, the report offered nothing of practical value to people to solve what is very much *their* problem as much as it is one for governments.

The Report was released at a Group of 20 (G-20) Labor and Employment Ministerial Meeting (LEMM) in Australia in September 2014. The Bank said that "an extra 600 million jobs need to be created worldwide by 2030 just to cope with the expanding population" (Iyengar, 2014)

Nigel Twose, senior director of the Jobs Cross-Cutting Solutions Area (CCSA) of the World Bank Group, said:

> There's little doubt there is a global jobs crisis. As this report makes clear, there is a shortage of jobs—and quality jobs. And equally disturbingly, we're also seeing wage and income inequality widening within many G-20 countries, although progress has been made in a few emerging economies, like Brazil and South Africa (AFP 2014).

He said that overall emerging market economies had done better than advanced G-20 countries in job creation, driven primarily by countries such as China and Brazil, but the overall outlook is bleak: "Current projections are dim. Challenging times loom large," he said in the typically understated way bureaucrats tend to describe things (AFP, 2014).

We should believe the facts . . . but which ones?

Mainstream media are so heavily influenced by government spin that we cannot take anything at face value. And this is why this report by the World Bank has to be taken seriously. The World Bank isn't beyond the influence of key stakeholders with their own agendas. And many have argued that the World Bank, which has had an American as its president ever since its creation in 1946, promotes a US-based world view.

Although the World Bank is not beyond criticism, truly, politicians don't control the World Bank. And that's the most important thing in our view. No one at the World Bank is trying to win votes from citizens. The leaders of the World Bank do not gain any benefit by telling people that things are better than they really are.

Fact: The real unemployment numbers

The G-20 report, compiled in collaboration with the Organisation for Economic Co-operation and Development (OECD) and International Labour Organization (ILO), reported that more than 100 million people were unemployed in G-20 economies, and *447 million* were considered "working poor," living on less than $2 (US) a day (G20 LEMM, 2014).

The report indicated that despite a modest economic recovery in 2013–14, global growth was expected to remain weak in the foreseeable future. There is risk that the economy could continue to weaken. The weak jobs markets were dampening consumer and business spending and investment.

This persistent slow growth will continue to dampen employment prospects, it said, warning that real wages had stagnated across many advanced G-20 nations and even fallen in some.

Nigel Twose again:

> There is no magic bullet to solve this jobs crisis,
> in emerging markets or advanced economies.
> We do know we need to create an extra 600
> million jobs worldwide by the year 2030 just to
> cope with the expanding population.
>
> That requires not just the leadership of minis-
> tries of labor but their active collaboration with
> all other ministries—a whole of government
> approach cutting across different ministries, and
> of course the direct and sustained involvement
> of the private sector. (AFP, 2014)

The G-20 leaders have called for each member country to develop growth strategies and employment action plans. They emphasize the need for coordinated and integrated public policies, along with resilient social protection systems, sustainable public finance, and well-regulated financial systems.

The report continued: "Coordinated policies in these areas are seen as the foundation for sustainable, job-creating economic growth."

So there we have it. The responsibility for solving the problem has been passed to national governments. And govern-ments have been urged to adopt a cross-departmental approach to create solutions. Given the nature of governmental silos and the painfully slow way in which government policies are formulated and implemented, your authors are not holding their breath for any big breakthroughs anytime soon.

Summary

At the writing of this book, in 2016, there are over 212 million unemployed people across the global landscape (International Labour Organization, 2015). We wrote this book for those people who are ready to take their future into their own hands and craft the plan that will ensure their future financial integrity.

This book cannot guarantee your career success, but it will give you insight and detailed action steps into the survival techniques everyone will need in the coming years.

WHERE ARE WE AND HOW DID WE GET HERE?

The first thing you should know

Part One of this book is about why jobs are disappearing faster than Western economies can create new ones.

But it's critical to understand that *jobs are not extinct,* and they will not become extinct in any of our lifetimes. Today and every day forward, in every state of the USA and other developed economies around the world, people are getting hired and starting new jobs. This includes growth businesses and contracting business sectors too. This includes all levels of jobs from intern to C-suite and everything in between, as well as every other sector.

Thousands and thousands of new jobs are being advertised every single day—week in and week out. Employers frequently report difficulties in filling vacancies. What is also happening is that jobs are becoming harder to land. Companies are using new methods to screen and rank candidates, and career progression is becoming less linear and less predictable. Most people are aware of this change. Few know how to react to it. Many unemployed jobseekers have applied for hundreds of jobs without success. They take this personal experience, combine it with the depressing headlines about the economy, and think that they may as well give up. They mistakenly decide that they cannot and will not be able to get hired. They believe they cannot progress to the next level of their career or they are unable to switch to a new one.

They are frustrated. It's not because this is an insoluble problem but simply because they don't know how to play by the new rules.

Jobs and careers are not going to simply disappear. They are just going to be different. People will continue to have great careers—provided they know how to change their approach to career management to accommodate these dramatic changes.

To do this, everyone needs to know what has changed and why. The wake of the 2008 crash and subsequent recession (the Great Recession) caused sweeping changes. Chief among those changes is that work and jobs have transformed so drastically that many people feel completely unequipped to cope.

We will shortly explain why the Great Recession in 2008 was not what caused this transformation. Other structural factors have been engines of change for much longer. So we begin this book by examining the Six Engines of Change which have created the crisis. This provides an essential foundation for understanding why the measures we recommend later in the book are critical for anyone who wishes to remain employable in the 21st century.

We are committed to your success

If you are reading this, you may be frustrated about your own career and worried about your prospects for the future. You are right to seek answers, and we hope this book provides an abundance of them.

We encourage you *not* to abandon hope. Just as thousands of people are losing their jobs, so thousands are being hired and advancing their careers as well. This book will help ensure that you are one of them.

Origins of the global jobs crisis
The 2008 Great Recession didn't cause the jobs crisis

The Great Recession of 2008 onward caused a lot of problems in the world. But one problem it didn't cause is the global jobs crisis. It certainly didn't help matters, but there are clues that the situation will not and cannot ever return to how it was *before* 2008.

In fact, the evidence is all around us. Consider the static or falling growth in real incomes. Have you noticed larger and larger wealth inequality? Have you heard the words *Quantitative Easing* (QE) and phrases like *the ongoing injection of liquidity into economies through central banks?* And biggest of all are the mountains of government debt around the world. (QE will be discussed in depth in a later section.)

For most people, these news briefs pass by as part of the daily din with little or no meaning to their personal lives. On the whole, growing government debt does not cause alarm to the average person trying to get through their day, week, or month.

We live under a misconception about the Great Recession. The real story of the 2008 financial collapse and subsequent recession isn't about greedy bankers, sleeping regulators or complacent politicians—although they all played their part. The story is bigger than all of them put together. It's about the transition of the whole developed world from one economic era to an entirely new one.

It is simply not true that all our financial woes were created by the Great Recession of 2008 and its aftermath. Yes, it's true that we've been going through possibly the worst recession in history. But the financial crisis wasn't the cause of this; it was a symptom of much bigger global transformations that have been advancing for decades.

Only if we understand the nature of this transformation can we figure out what each of us will have to do in the coming years to ensure that we don't become victims. Many of us have suffered enough already from the economic collapse. But the collapse wasn't a singular event. It was a symptom of a much bigger problem; we are in a postindustrial age, and the free market economy that we are all accustomed to is struggling to function.

While 2008 and its aftermath brought untold wealth destruction to many, the future will be just as painful to many more of us. This will be especially true if we don't individually figure out our own survival plan now.

We first need to look at what's been going on and why.

Who is really to blame for the recession?

In 2008, the world changed. It involved events that to many, seemed completely unthinkable. Lehman Brothers' bankruptcy triggered crisis across the world's largest financial institutions, and the whole global monetary system was at risk of unraveling, with unimaginable consequences. Only frantic government and central bank interventions prevented a total economic meltdown. Most people have no idea how close we came to global economic collapse.

The world entered the worst recession since the 1930s. But unlike the 1930s, eight years later, we are still stuck in this one.

How did this happen? It's tempting to adopt over simplistic, knee-jerk explanations. People were too greedy. Lenders were too careless. Big bonuses encouraged unethical and even illegal practices. Politicians were self-serving. There is plenty of evidence of all these realities, of course, but they are not at the root of the problem. They are merely symptoms of deeper fundamental changes in the world.

Credit and borrowing underpin the whole of the world economy today. Credit is not in itself a bad thing. It can serve as a useful means of paying big bills through smaller, more affordable repayments. The trouble is that the world has become addicted to credit. It is an addiction that we cannot break—without some really nasty and unpleasant side effects.

The very word *credit* is an oxymoron. We're talking about debt—personal debt, business debt, government debt. All debt is essentially exchanging future income for cash today and paying a charge for the privilege. Debt is okay provided it is easily manageable. But when it becomes unmanageable, it inevitably spirals out of control, with horrible consequences.

A little debt is fine for the jobs market. With a little debt, employers can reasonably grow their businesses and create new jobs. A lot of debt promotes short-term thinking. It inhibits spending. An employer with a heavy debt burden naturally seeks to restrain their headcount and freezes wages. But debt isn't just used by businesses. It's become the default method of payment for millions of individuals, employers, and governments around the world. Again: people, employers, and governments borrow money to pay their debt, and in doing so, increase their debt burden.

The world's debt crisis has massive implications for jobs and careers. And none of these implications are good. Rising debt impacts every level of a society:

- Rising *personal debt* means people have to earn more to pay for it.
- Rising *business debt* places greater pressure on business owners and increases business costs, which are passed on to consumers through higher prices.
- Rising *government debt* forces reductions in government services to its citizens.

A debt-burdened economy forces employers to attempt to do the same or more work with fewer people who are paid less. Businesses don't care where these people are in the world if they can get the job done for the lowest possible price. So the offshoring of jobs from domestic workforces to cheaper workers in other countries became an increasing feature of business practices from the mid 1980s.

The next partner for business in its relentless quest for lower costs is technology. Why pay people to do the work, if you can do the same thing better, faster, and cheaper with machines? The cost associated with technology continues to decrease. This opens the floodgates for thousands of new innovative businesses that are nibbling away at the established corporate giants. These "disruptive innovators" are often hot topics for business schools and conferences. What the media fails to report is that they are a catastrophe for jobs.

In essence, technology has three impacts on business and competition:

- It removes the barriers to entry in many business sectors—i.e., the ability to enter a market requires fewer people and less equipment, premises, and capital. This means that big companies have more competition, and small businesses can compete.
- It makes production capability more widely available to more people. Advances such as computing power and 3D printing mean that one person is capable of production that previously could be accomplished only by the greater resources within large organizations.
- Smaller employers are now able to compete through lower operating costs and flexibility in product offerings and their participation in global e-commerce via the Internet.

Essentially these businesses, employing a small number of people, are relentlessly eating away at many of the world's biggest employers. When a global employer closes a division, thousands of jobs can be lost. Yet the businesses that have disrupted them typically employ just a handful of people. We will examine these topics in more detail later, but here we will stick with the topic of the financial conditions that we can expect to see in the near future. These will shape the economic conditions that will determine the outlook for jobs.

How central banks made the 2008 Great Recession possible

The enablers of the 2008 collapse are in the shadows, or at least so low-profile and mysterious to most of us that they attract little attention from the public. They are the central banks. A central bank is the national institution that controls the money supply within a given nation. It sets interest rates, acts as the lender of last resort, and issues currency. It is usually tasked with goals such as ensuring that inflation remains within acceptable limits.

Understanding how the actions of central banks affect jobs is essential if you are going to maximize your career resilience in the toughest economic conditions the world has experienced for decades.

The central bank in the US is the Federal Reserve. In the UK, it's the Bank of England. In Europe, it's the European Central Bank. The central banks lend money to financial institutions, including commercial banks. They also control the lending rules around what bankers call "fractional reserves."

What this practice means is that only a fraction of a bank's activities is backed by actual cash.

Let's say that I want to buy a house for $200,000. I go to my local or national bank to borrow the money. The bank has received a "loan" from the central bank, which they are using to lend the money to me. Anyone who has purchased a house knows that the bank doesn't hand over the $200,000 in cash so I can then hand it over to the owner. The bank doesn't actually have to have that money on hand—because the rules set by the Federal Reserve only mandate that my bank needs to have a *fraction* of the money they lend in actual cash.

Let's say that the fractional reserve set by the central bank is 5 percent. This means the bank only has to have $10,000 in its reserve to fund my loan for $200,000. So with a fractional reserve of 5 percent, institutions can actually lend *twenty times* the deposits that they hold. Put another way, for every dollar lent by a commercial bank, ninety-five cents is "created" out of thin air. Central banks are effectively fabricating illusionary wealth via the commercial banks that multiply every dollar from the central bank twentyfold.

The Federal Reserve has injected trillions of dollars into US commercial banks since 2008 (Collins, 2015). All of them make loans to various businesses, collect the principal and interest on the loans, and then use their profit to pay back the central bank and make other loans. And with each rotation of every dollar, the fractional reserve rules allow the twentyfold multiplication to occur. The illusionary wealth spirals and compounds.

The premise behind fractional reserves is that banks are responsible and prudent institutions that merit the trust and confidence of most or all of their depositors. It assumes that nothing could possibly happen to cause many or all of the depositors to withdraw all of their money at the same time.

That we should all implicitly trust the banks seems like a crazy notion when we remember that there have been plenty of bank runs throughout history. For the record, these include:

- The Dutch Tulip Manias (1634–1637)
- The British South Sea Bubble (1717–1719)
- The French Mississippi Company (1717–1720)
- The Post-Napoleonic Depression (1815–1830)
- The Great Depression (1929–1939)
- The Great Recession (2008–?)

So we can see that the collapse of 2008 was just the latest in a series of banking failures and economic catastrophes throughout history.

Post-1945, in an attempt to restore growth to nations shattered by the effects of two world wars, the rules regarding these fractional reserves were progressively relaxed. These softer fractional reserve rules caused an explosion in lending. Had the rules been tighter, a lending explosion would have been unlikely, and we might have avoided a financial crisis.

With hindsight today, it seems incredible that the idea of fractional reserves could persist, but it did and it still does. And no one is talking about abandoning the fractional reserve system. Even with all those catastrophes, this system is still viewed by governments and central banks as a reasonable means to support their economies by enabling businesses to borrow money to grow and consumers to spend.

Requirements have been changed since 2008. The main drivers of this are called the Basel Accords I, II, and III, which have sought to apply more stringent capital reserve requirements to commercial banks in order to increase their solvency. These changes, requiring slightly higher capital reserves and greater risk mitigation, will be discussed in greater length in the next section.

The relatively small improvements imposed by the Basel Accords are a sensible move by government to lessen the potential impact of another financial crisis on their treasuries. However, they do very little to lessen the risk of another financial crisis.

Even with the Basel Accords, there has only been a modest increase in financial stability. So the outlook for future economic crises has not improved much. And this means that the vulnerability of jobs to future economic crises has not been reduced either.

We simply cannot ignore the global financial situation when we are thinking about our future ability to earn a living. It is completely realistic and rational to anticipate that financial instability will be spreading more chaos across the economy again soon, destroying still more jobs.

Governments are mortgaging our future

Do you think your work is solely for your benefit? It isn't so. Like it or not, unless we are working in the black economy (a.k.a. the underground economy, such as illegal drug trafficking), everyone is working for the government. Western democracy encourages politicians to try to make voters happy. But politicians don't get popular by spending responsibly when it comes to public services. Instead, politicians get popular by building more schools, providing better health care, cutting taxes, providing more policemen to keep us safe . . . the list goes on and on. But voters are hard to please when the government is spending money faster than the population can earn and pay taxes. This is where the central banks become super useful to governments in the form of Quantitative Easing (QE).

How Quantitative Easing works and why it's used

A central bank will make an arrangement with a government in the form of an IOU. The central bank provides extra money (liquidity) into the system as a loan, in exchange for a promise from the government that money will be paid back. The central bank issues a bill (an invoice) for the amount of the loan. In return, the government gives the bank a promise to pay back the money from its future income. This is called a bond.

Future income? What is the future income of a government? Taxes! So through the use of bonds, a government plans to pay back the IOU through the taxes of its citizens. In essence, the government is mortgaging the future wealth of the nation. Just as homeowners plan to pay off their mortgage with future earnings, the government plans to pay off the loan through the future work and earnings of its population.

But there is one *big* difference. The homeowner keeps the house in good condition and can sell the home if needed, to pay off the loan. However, the government spends the money outright. The only thing left to pay back the loan if there is a problem is to raise taxes. Today, there *is* a problem, a big one. The loans are due, but the incomes of the people have diminished with the faltering economy, and they really can't afford higher taxes.

Repeatedly, governments have borrowed more and more money. Just as with a mortgage, where the bank allows the homeowner to pay only the interest (and not the capital) on the loan for a specified time, nations have opted to do the same thing. They pay only the interest on the loan. But what happens when the monetary value of what the nation produces (Gross Domestic Product) is less than the interest payments on the loans that the government has agreed to pay?

Case Study: Sam needs $10,000.

Let's say Sam is totally broke and needs $10,000 to expand his business to bring in higher revenue. Sam goes to ten of his business partners and says, "If you will loan me $1,000 today, I'll pay you $1,400 in two years." They know that Sam's business has been successful and has shown consistent growth—so they agree. Sam spends the money he receives to expand his business. In two years, he will need $14,000 to pay off his debt. This is his bond. Sam was gambling that, with the improvements to the business, he would be more profitable after two years and able to repay the loans.

Now let's say it's two years later, and Sam can't pay off his bonds. His investors are pressuring him to pay up. Once again, Sam gets a loan to pay off his debtors, pushing his business into greater debt. This happens over and over again. Eventually Sam is in so much debt that there is no hope that he will ever pay it off. What's worse, his business isn't doing so well, and his good name is no longer "good." No one wants to lend Sam any more money. Creditors are unwilling to continue to invest in Sam's business.

On the other side of all this, Sam's creditors are doing the same thing. As a matter of fact, everywhere Sam looks, it's the same story. The idea that there is any value, either in Sam's business or his credibility, is an illusion.

The bigger problem is that Sam is not an individual or a company. He is a government. His friends are banks and large corporations. He can't just tell his creditors that he is filing for bankruptcy and lay everybody off—that would be nearly everyone in the country! And . . . his creditors have done the same thing. So he does what all governments have done (but what people and businesses cannot): he turns to his central bank and issues even more bonds in exchange for more credit.

The term "bond-bingeing" has been used to describe this situation. A government can simply provide the central bank that loans them the money with a promise to pay. The government's credit rating dictates the interest rate they pay. So since poorly performing countries' bonds are considered riskier, governments with poor credit have to pay more interest than others.

Our Western political system provides a selection of unpalatable choices for governments when debt is at critically high levels. None of the options are attractive. They can:

- Spend less on services
- Raise taxes
- Try to stimulate growth by cutting interest rates

But whereas cutting interest rates can help momentarily, wholesome economic growth is usually painfully slow. It takes years for real economic growth to convert into government incomes. So we end up with political hesitation, compromise, and public frustration. Does this sound familiar?

The bottom line for jobs is that regardless of who is in the White House or any other government leadership role, or what decisions they make, there are simply no good options left.

CRITICAL SUMMARY POINT: This is why today, in the current economic climate, very few of us can rely on government policy or action to make any significant impact on our job and career prospects. But we *can* take responsibility for our own future by proactively managing our personal revenue streams through career management principles that we are going to show you later in this book.

How the rich are getting richer

Governments are not just promising to use our future work to pay for the loans associated with Quantitative Easing (QE);

they are making the rich richer in the process. This is one of the unforeseen consequences of Quantitative Easing.

Quantitative Easing has helped avoid total collapse, but it's a medicine with nasty side effects for ordinary people. In August 2012, the Bank of England issued a report stating that its quantitative easing policies had benefited mainly the wealthy. The report said that the QE program had boosted the value of stocks and bonds by 26 percent or about £970 billion. About 40 percent of those gains went to the richest 5 percent of British households. Dhaval Joshi of BCA Research wrote that "QE cash ends up overwhelmingly in profits, thereby exacerbating already extreme income inequality and the consequent social tensions that arise from it" (Stewart, 2011).

Economist Anthony Randazzo of the Reason Foundation wrote that QE "is fundamentally a regressive redistribution program that has been boosting wealth for those already engaged in the financial sector or those who already own homes, but passing little along to the rest of the economy. It is a primary driver of income inequality" (Frank, 2013).

About one year later, in May 2013, the president of the Federal Reserve Bank of Dallas, Richard Fisher, said that "cheap money" (lending money at very low rates of interest) has made rich people richer, but has not done anything much to help working Americans.

Most of the financial assets in America are owned by the wealthiest 5 percent of Americans. According to Fed data, the top 5 percent own 60 percent of the nation's individually held financial assets. They own 82 percent of individually held stocks and over 90 percent of individually held bonds. So as

Quantitative Easing caused the rise in the stock market, these individuals profited. They became richer.

But the majority of people have not invested in stocks and bonds, and they are getting poorer with the weakening economy. As this happens, they are less able and less inclined to borrow money. And this is exactly what we see happening. As the national debt rises through borrowed money for QE, the volume of personal debt has been falling.*

How the poor are getting poorer

An additional factor is contributing to the situation. Do you remember the "housing bubble"? The banking industry lent money to eager homebuyers, even when they couldn't demonstrate they could pay back the loans. It was all smoke and mirrors because the banks knew that the future income of the homebuyers might not be sufficient to pay back the loans. But they lent the money anyway because they had constructed elaborate portfolio risk mitigation strategies, which proved to be entirely unreliable. The failure of these "instruments" sparked the 2008 economic collapse.

As a consequence, the Basel Committee on Banking Supervision (BCBS) issued what is known as the Basel Accords. These contain recommendations to banks regarding the regulation of lending practices. These regulations tried to protect consumers from getting loans they could not pay back. It also made it more difficult for a homebuyer to get a loan.

---

* As of 2017, personal debt has been rising again through the growth of credit card and car finance. Lending rules for these are less tight than for home loans; a loophole which is stoking up a future debt crisis.

If you or someone you know has tried to purchase a home since 2008; it is likely that a mountain of paperwork was required to ensure that the mortgage could be paid back. Every financial detail of the mortgage transaction, every penny paid for the down payment, and every detail of future income is now carefully scrutinized and verified by the bank. The risk of lending money to every individual is carefully assessed. Consequently, for many people, borrowing money is no longer an option.

The important point as we move forward in this discussion is that it has become harder and harder for the everyday person or the small business to get a loan, while governments are printing more and more money and borrowing freely.

In the UK (largely but not entirely because of the bank bailouts), government debt has risen exponentially in the wake of 2008, while private debt has been falling (Pettinger, 2013):

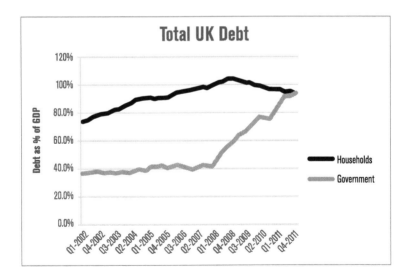

The system makes it much easier for governments to borrow than to save

To say "bond-bingeing" has become a bad habit is an understatement. In the US today, government borrowing has become a debt crisis. During a two-week period between September 30 and October 17, 2013, much of the US government infrastructure was forced into shutdown due to the inability of Congress to agree about how the costs of the Affordable Care Act (Obamacare) could be met.

In a financial crisis, you'd expect that a responsible government would look for every way possible to reduce spending. And yes, they attempt to do this—but not very successfully. Every proposal to reduce spending prompts a counterargument that it's unfair, unpopular, or impossible or that it will lead to extra costs elsewhere. And this is where our governments fail us.

Unlike businesses, which will act fast, ruthlessly slash costs, and do whatever they can to remain solvent, governments are huge, unwieldy bureaucracies. And every cost-cutting proposal becomes bogged down in debate, argument, and ultimately delay and compromise. Plus, when all else fails, they can always turn to their central bank . . . and borrow more money . . . secured against the future work of their citizens.

While central banks have the power to "print" money, it's a mistake to assume that this is either dollar bills flying off printing presses or that much of this extra cash actually trickles down to people and businesses. First, no actual printing happens at all. The extra cash doesn't even exist in the form of hard currency—it's more or less a simple electronic "adjustment."

While these events typically involve billions of dollars, most of it finds its way, first, into commercial banks. Then these banks lend the money to other banks and financial institutions, which, in turn, lend it to other financial institutions. And at every step, because of fractional reserves, each billion from the central bank is multiplied many times over. It's a sleight of hand—a neat trick for governments to create the illusion of improvement. And it's why, despite endless amounts of QE and trillions of dollars injected, almost none of it has had any material effect on the lives and incomes of working people.

US government debt is in crisis as it continues to soar out of control. In 2008, when the economy tanked, government

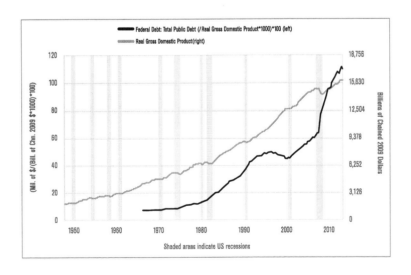

spending also increased with each quantitative easing program. The Gross Domestic Product (GDP) growth recovered but at a horrendous price, as government debt took off like a rocket (FRED Economic Research, n.d.).

In other words, although the country was increasing the monetary value of its services and products (GDP), the government was spending it faster than the value was increasing.

Total US public debt in 2015 was $18.2 trillion (Patton, 2015). That's $154,161 for every taxpayer. US debt is 31.3 percent of all the debt in the world. GDP is one of the primary gauges of a nation's economic health. A "prudent" ratio of GDP to national debt is 60 percent (Chowdhury, n.d.). In the US, government debt has risen to over 70 percent of GDP.

Case Study: Serena and the US Debt

Let's make another analogy. Suppose Serena earns $100,000 a year. And she has total assets of $500,000 in the form of the equity in her house, her car, and the rest of her belongings. For most people $100,000 is a comfortable income. But Serena has repeatedly borrowed against her assets, and now she has amassed total debts of $700,000. So even if Serena sold everything she has, she wouldn't come close to being able to pay off her debt. The moment one large unexpected bill arrives, she'll be in big trouble.

This is the situation in most developed economies around the world today; the incomes are completely inadequate to support the liabilities. But every time there is a turn for the worse, and with no real alternatives, governments resort to yet more bond-bingeing. And so the cycle continues.

Other Western economies are not far behind. In the UK, government debt per person is $32,553. In Germany, it is $31,945. In France, it is $31,915; in Italy, $37,956. In the most struggling Western economies, the situation is even worse. Greek debt per person is $40,486, a staggering 161 percent of Greece's GDP.

Why economic recovery won't restore incomes

This wouldn't be so frightening if Western economies were showing an improvement in household incomes and earnings. But this isn't happening. *In fact, in the United States, the reverse has been happening for over 40 years.* In other words, in real terms, the incomes of everyday people are getting smaller. Despite rising productivity in the US, real household income has hardly grown at all since 1973!

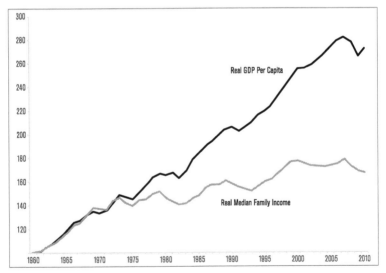

http://bit.ly/24YiQpU

22

What we see here is critical. The historical and vital connection between GDP and household income has broken—permanently.

And this reality has nothing to do with the financial collapse and the recession. It has little or nothing to do with party politics. It's not about left versus right or capitalism versus socialism. The reality has been staring us in the face for 40 years or more. There are two parts to the situation:

1. GDP is going up.
2. Average household income is going down.

The Problem, Part 1: GDP is going up

As technology continues to accelerate productivity, it relentlessly reduces production costs and delivers greater productivity. It also lessens the need for human labor. But there is absolutely no reason to believe that future GDP growth will result in increased household incomes. It is perverse! (The opposite is also true: falls in GDP also cannot push household incomes higher). As technology endlessly increases productivity, so we are getting more and more done with less and less human effort. And less work by people means naturally less pay.

Companies are reinvesting their gains in more technology rather than in people. Compared to machines, people are slower, more expensive, and more difficult to manage. Machines don't need to be paid, and they rarely make mistakes, complain, or go on vacation.

Machines also have an insidious side effect. Although they create work for those who have the technical skills to develop, use, and maintain them (an often transitory minority), they also destroy jobs for a majority of people whose skills are usurped by them.

So right now, we see a rise in productivity, the GDP. But this also brings a relentless downward pressure on jobs and incomes. Technology is fueling corporate profits, but little or none of this is finding its way into the pockets of employees. Worse, it isn't even supporting government programs to fund welfare benefits. That's because of the toxic combination of massive government debt (which demands constant prioritization for repayment) and the ability of large corporations to minimize their tax liabilities by means of complex offshore accounting structures.

The Problem, Part 2: Average household income is going down

So the culprits are business, government, and monetary systems. In the West, society has certain expectations of these systems. We expect that as we work hard and produce more, we will earn more. We expect that increased GDP will deliver higher pay and greater tax income for the government, which in turn will deliver more and better public services. And we expect that our governments and central banks will provide a stable and secure financial environment free from risks and shocks.

However, at this point in time, these expectations of what the system can and should deliver have completely outstripped its abilities to meet those expectations.

Case Study

Marlene has worked hard during her career. She has been a technical welder in the medical technology manufacturing field. Highly skilled and meticulous, she is one of the highest producers on her team. Advances in technology brought changes to her company, and soon, more people were laid off because robotic automation was able to accomplish the same work. Fewer people were needed. At first, Marlene's job was reduced to part-time, reducing her household income and eliminating her benefits. Meanwhile the company was able to cut prices, sell more, and make higher profits . . . at least for a while.

Competitors also automated their processes. They took out loans to implement greater automation, believing that without the cost of so many employees, and with the ability to increase their production, they too would be able to cut costs, sell more, and increase their profit.

However, these optimistic expectations proved to be erroneous. In combination, the companies were producing more products than the market needed. The only way they could prop up sales was to lower their prices. This created a price war, with constant competitive price-cutting in a struggle for market share. With reduced sales and income, some companies could no longer pay their loans. They went bust, and thousands of jobs were lost. The remaining companies breathed a sigh of relief. As the dust settled, there was no place for the people who had lost their jobs; automation ensured that *those* jobs could never return.

There is no way for companies to catch up because again and again, technology will reduce the cost of production and the need for human effort. As markets become saturated with goods, prices will be lowered, and sooner or later, company revenues will decrease as well.

Consequently, we have arrived at a place where stagnation is the principal characteristic of most Western economies. And that's a very bad place for citizens to be when their survival depends on their ability to earn a living.

Hope is coming

To cope with this situation, we all need a strategy. And to have a strategy, we first need to understand the environment. Next, we'll take a look at what is killing jobs and how. Then we will be able to show you how to identify new opportunities that are surfacing. Finally, we will follow with a process to manage your future so you stay ahead of the curve and maintain an income stream for you and your family.

The Six Engines of Change

As discussed in the previous section, while monetary and economic policies are struggling to remedy the aftermath of the Great Recession, economics and government policies are not the main structural reasons that jobs have been disappearing.

There were inherent weaknesses within financial regulation, government, and monetary policies that triggered the 2008 financial crash. Yes, these failures destroyed jobs, but other forces are at work that have been killing jobs for much longer. These forces will continue to cause jobs to disappear even if governments and central banks can restore real growth to our economies and households.

There are six engines of change for jobs in the world today. Not one of them is connected with the Great Recession. They can be divided into two groups. The first group involve choices employers are making. We can anticipate that employers will continue making choices toward these trends:

1. Globalization and offshoring

2. Technology, artificial intelligence and robotics

3. Disruptive business models

The second group are beyond the control of any organization or employer:

4. Education and the speed of institutional change

5. Demographics and the aging population

6. Fiscal policy

Each of these brings problems and opportunities for those of us who are seeking to secure our careers and future incomes. Like most complex problems, if we break things down and unpack the details, then we can start to understand how to solve the problem. So let's look at each of these change agents in turn.

Engine of Change No. 1: Globalization and offshoring

About 35 years ago, Western businesses started sending low-skilled manufacturing jobs abroad. By the late 1980s this was well established. And it grew and grew and grew. This mass-migration of jobs was always in one direction: away from developed countries to places where workers with adequate skills were much less expensive.

Lower labor costs were the biggest driver—but only at first. For many firms, their very survival was at stake; new competitors, often overseas, were undercutting them on price. This usually involved closing plants in America and Western Europe and moving production to new factories in China, Mexico, India, Taiwan, or Eastern Europe. Suddenly, "Made in the USA" and "Made in England" became unusual labels on the goods we all buy.

Initially, businesses, governments and consumers could only see the upside to globalization:

- For workers in low-cost countries, it provided jobs and improved their standards of living.

- Rich-world workers were able to leave the boring and tedious work to someone else.

- Western consumers were able to buy goods at much lower prices than if production was at home.

- For companies, lower labor costs brought higher profits.

The trouble is that while these are all good things in small doses, what happens when the number of jobs leaving an economy are significantly greater than the ability to create new ones at home?

Many of America's greatest companies have left for good
In February 2011, Barack Obama joined Silicon Valley's "captains of tech" for dinner. Each guest had been asked to

bring a question for the president. As Steve Jobs of Apple spoke, Obama interrupted him with a question. He asked Jobs, "What would it take to make iPhones in the United States?" (Duhigg and Bradsher, NYT, 2012).

Originally, Apple had been able to boast that all its products were made in America. Today, few are. Almost all of the 70 million iPhones, 30 million iPads, and 59 million other products Apple sold the previous year (2010) were manufactured overseas.

"Why can't that work come home?" Obama asked.

Jobs' reply was stark and uncompromising. "Those jobs aren't coming back," he said.

The unpalatable truth is that Apple and many of its peers are not nearly as committed to creating American jobs as the previous generations of US industrial giants were.

The capacity to manufacture product in the US has become largely obsolete. This is because factories in Asia can scale up and down faster. They have more flexible workforces due to lower costs of living, which means they can be paid less than US workers. Further, Asian supply chains have now massively surpassed what's possible in the US. In other words, they can get the resources they need faster and cheaper than in the US. The result is that much of America's manufacturing capacity has become largely obsolete.

We might think of ourselves as American, German, or British. We might think that we should be able to find work not too far from where we live. But this idea too is obsolete. Today, we are all integrated into a global economy. We have to think globally because work and trade are global.

To some people this is an exciting prospect. For others, it is truly terrifying.

But the good news is that thinking globally doesn't necessarily mean we need to spend our lives globetrotting or relocating to foreign cultures or countries. It just means thinking differently about where our work and career opportunities may be found.

Job security was traditionally greatest with large employers. Today even these stalwarts of business are reorganizing, restructuring, downsizing, and breaking up faster than ever before. They are being disrupted by technologies and smaller businesses, and *these* disrupters do not create many jobs.

Case Study: How many Apples are needed to make one General Motors? 10 actually . . .

Apple employs 43,000 people in the United States and 20,000 overseas, a small fraction of the over 400,000 American workers at General Motors in the 1950s, or the hundreds of thousands at General Electric in the 1980s.

Apple's decision to manufacture overseas reveals why the success of some prominent companies has not translated into large numbers of domestic jobs. "Companies once felt an obligation to support American workers, even when it wasn't the best financial choice," said Betsey Stevenson, formerly the chief economist at the US Labor Department. "That's disappeared. Profits and efficiency have trumped generosity."

"Apple's an example of why it's so hard to create middle-class jobs in the US now," said Jared Bernstein, formerly an economic adviser to the White House. "If it's the pinnacle of capitalism, we should be worried."

"We sell iPhones in over a hundred countries," a current Apple executive said. "We don't have an obligation to solve America's problems. Our only obligation is making the best product possible" (Duhigg and Bradsher, NYT, 2012).

Summary: Globalization and offshoring

So business says it's not their problem, and government doesn't know how to solve it. And just like two squabbling children, neither will accept any responsibility, let alone ownership. And therein lies the crux of the problem: business will keep on doing what business does—chasing profits. And government will keep on doing what government does—borrowing money, raising taxes for sure. But you, the reader, can add to the list as you see fit.

Consequently, we have to create our own personal solution. We have to be our own personal economist, marketer, and recruiter agent and have a strategic plan for our career management. That's what this book is about.

So we cannot look to government for solutions, nor can we expect businesses to suddenly have an attack of conscience and start bringing jobs back home. The competition for work is now global. Some younger and more mobile professionals have responded to this situation with direct action. They have simply migrated overseas. This solves two problems at once. First, they go to where the work is. Second, because this is often in countries where costs of living are much lower, they can enjoy a higher standard of living than they could at home.

We understand though that for most people, especially workers with families to support, such a decision is overwhelmingly difficult, impractical, or both. So the good news is that emigrating is not going to be part of the solution we advocate later in the book. Thinking globally is simply not as mind-boggling as it might at first seem. Communications technology continually advances, and employers increasingly recognize that remote working arrangements give them access to a much larger pool of talent. Together, this means that for more and more people, working for overseas employers without emigrating is becoming more and more common.

Engine of change No. 2: Technology, artificial intelligence, and robotics

The computerization of work is one of the most commonly quoted reasons for the destruction of jobs. If you understand the process by which this happens, you will be better able to anticipate when and if your current employment may be vulnerable to elimination.

The future's here, ready or not.

Brynjolfsson and McAfee, in their book, *The Second Machine Age,* paint an optimistic picture of the future. As the full impact of digital technologies is felt, they predict we will realize an immense bounty in the form of dazzling personal technology, advanced infrastructure, and near-boundless access to cultural items that enrich our lives.

Yet even Brynjolfsson and McAfee admit that amid this bounty, wrenching change will also occur (Brynjolfsson and McAfee, 2014). Professions of all kinds, from lawyers to truck drivers, will be relentlessly disrupted and downsized. Companies will be forced to transform or close down. Will they spot the need to transform quickly enough to respond? We think it's safe to predict that some will, and some won't and will suffer the consequences. Recent economic indicators already reflect this shift; wages are falling even as productivity and GDP improve.

We don't doubt the guarantee of technological transformation. What we doubt is the capability of organizations to transform fast enough to keep up, to say nothing of institutions and legal systems. True, technology is enabling things to be made and done faster and cheaper than ever before. At the same time, this speed is outpacing people's ability to extract enough money from the system to live.

The challenge of rapid change

Brynjolfsson and McAfee recognize that to adapt, society must change rapidly. The trouble is that no society in history has ever changed rapidly without the occurrence of some destructive event like war, revolution, or economic collapse. Gradual deterioration just isn't an agent of change.

The changes Brynjolfsson and McAfee claim are needed include:

1. Revamping education so that it prepares people for the next economy instead of the last one,

2. Designing new collaborations that pair brute processing power with human ingenuity, and,

3. Embracing policies that make sense in a radically transformed landscape (Brynjolfsson and McAfee, 2014).

Speed and adaptability are no longer just desirable; they are essential in the 21st century. The pace of change cannot be chosen by any organization; rather it is thrust upon all of us. Organizations must embrace this new economic reality or they will die. People must adapt to it too, or they will risk perpetual obsolescence.

This creates a whole new world of economic winners and losers. The winners will be those who are ahead of the curve and who can adapt fast enough to avoid being blindsided. The losers will be those who cling to obsolete concepts of what career success looks like and how to achieve it.

The research by Oxford University academics Carl Benedikt Frey and Michael A. Osborne examines how susceptible jobs are to computerization. Their paper is titled *The Future of Employment: How Susceptible are Jobs to Computerisation?* (Frey and Osborne, 2013). Frey and Osborne developed a model which examined the current and anticipated capabilities of technology and then compared the tasks involved in carrying out over 700 different jobs. This enabled them to rank each job by its vulnerability to being reduced or eliminated by technology in the future.

Of course, robots and IT systems are still unable to match the depth and breadth of human perception. Basic pattern recognition is reasonably mature. And although it is enabled by the development of sophisticated algorithms, sensors, and lasers, significant challenges still remain for more complex perceptive tasks. So some jobs are at high risk. Others are still relatively immune.

Computers are not so good at identifying objects and their properties in a cluttered visual field; that's why we are forced to put up with those annoying Captchas when we navigate website forms. Similarly, tasks that involve close human interaction in an unstructured work environment make jobs less susceptible to computerization.

11 least at-risk jobs (to a point)

According to Frey and Osborne (2013), some of the least at-risk jobs are therefore:

- Recreational therapists
- Supervisors of mechanics, installers, and repairers
- Mental health and substance abuse social workers
- Occupational therapists
- Social workers
- Dieticians and nutritionists
- Choreographers
- Physicians and surgeons
- Psychologists
- Dentists
- Elementary school teachers

But even these jobs are *indirectly* at risk. Although the whole of a job may be currently impossible for a machine to replicate, *parts of that job* may easily be replaced or aided by technology. This fact in turn means that fewer people are needed to deliver the same amount of work.

It's important to remember that business has a habit of quickly finding ways around current technological limitations. If a human task cannot be replicated *exactly* by a machine, then why not just adapt the task so it can be?

The point is that although machines may be perceived as "limited", this problem can sometimes be sidestepped by clever task design. For example, Kiva Systems, acquired by Amazon.com in 2012, solved the problem of warehouse navigation for its robots by simply placing bar-code stickers on the floor, informing the robots of their precise location on the floor and the location of other robotic traffic. Problem solved! . . . And fewer humans needed.

30 most at-risk jobs

(According to Frey and Osborne, 2013)

- Legal secretaries
- Radio operators
- Drivers/sales workers
- Claims adjusters, examiners, and investigators
- Parts salespersons
- Credit Analysts
- Milling and planing machine setters, operators, and tenders, metal and plastic

- Shipping, receiving, and traffic clerks
- Procurement clerks
- Packaging and filling machine operators and tenders
- Etchers and engravers
- Tellers
- Umpires, referees, and other sports officials
- Insurance appraisers, auto damage
- Loan officers
- Order clerks
- Brokerage clerks
- Insurance claims and policy processing clerks
- Timing device assemblers and adjusters
- Data entry keyers
- Library technicians
- New accounts clerks
- Tax preparers
- Cargo and freight agents
- Watch repairers
- Insurance underwriters
- Mathematical technicians
- Sewers, hand
- Title examiners, abstractors, and searchers
- Telemarketers

This isn't just our opinion. Multiple and diverse organizations are reporting the same thing:

Manpower states that despite the recession, 31 percent of employers struggle to find qualified workers because of "a talent mismatch between workers' qualifications and the specific skill sets and combinations of skills employers want" (Manpower Group Talent Shortage Survey, 2012).

The American Management Corporation says that employers want workers who can think critically, solve problems creatively, innovate, collaborate, and communicate (American Management Association, 2010).

The National Association of Manufacturers reports, "Today's skill shortages are extremely broad and deep, cutting across industry sectors and impacting more than 80% of companies surveyed. This human capital performance gap threatens our nation's ability to compete . . . [and] is emerging as our nation's most critical business issue" (National Association of Manufacturers, 2005).

The National Academies claim that "The danger exists that Americans may not know enough about science, technology, or mathematics to contribute significantly to, or fully benefit from, the knowledge-based economy that is already taking shape around us" (21st Century Skill Research, 2016).

The New York Times reports that low-skilled workers are being laid off and "turned away at the factory door and increasingly joining the swelling ranks of the long-term unemployed . . . ." This issue results from a disparity between the skills that workers have and those that employers need (Rich, 2010).

Summary: Technology, artificial intelligence, and robotics

This destruction of jobs is sometimes called the third (or even fourth!) industrial revolution, the knowledge economy, or the new machine age. It shows no sign of letting up. This situation creates a whole new set of challenges for everyone who wants to earn a living in these tough times. We need new solutions, and we need to take personal ownership of our own countermeasures.

Engine of change No. 3: Disruptive business models

Disruptive business models have been getting a substantial amount of media coverage. New technologies have lowered the barriers for small businesses who can now compete with big business. Consequently, new tech-based disruptive businesses are springing up by the thousands. Because they are "jobs-lite" (they need very few employees), they have the ability to quickly increase and decrease their production to meet market demand; that is, they can scale easily with the market. Further, their business models also have the flexibility to accomplish rapid changes in their product offerings. This in turn facilitates their ability to accommodate ever-changing customer needs.

In January 2016, the Union Bank of Switzerland (UBS) produced a report which dealt with the main theme for the World Economic Forum conference at Davos, entitled "Extreme automation and connectivity: The global, regional, and investment implications of the Fourth Industrial Revolution."

The UBS report set out to forecast the impacts of current trends in technology, markets, business, and politics. They sought to provide a view of the economic outlook for different countries around the globe. Here is a quote from the introduction:

> Previous industrial revolutions have been driven by rapid advances in automation and connectivity, starting with the technologies that launched the First Industrial Revolution in 18th century England through to the exponential increases in computing power of recent decades. The Fourth Industrial Revolution is based on the same two forces. The first is extreme automation, the product of a growing role for robotics *and artificial intelligence* in business, government and private life. The second, extreme connectivity, annihilates distance and time as obstacles to ever deeper, faster communication between and among humans and machines.
>
> These changes will have very different effects on nations, businesses and individuals. Automation will continue to put downward pressure on the wages of the low skilled and is starting to impinge on the employment prospects of middle skilled workers.
>
> By contrast the potential returns to highly skilled and more adaptable workers are increasing.
>
> Among corporations, a wide range of traditional businesses—especially those that act as

intermediaries—can be expected to suffer. Many
labor-intensive firms should be *able to boost profit
margins as they substitute costly workers for cheaper
robots or intelligent software* (emphasis added).
(UBS, 2016)

Now we are getting to the real problem. So called "traditional businesses" are ones that have successfully grown over many decades and continue to employ lots of people. And yes, they are shrinking, automating, and collapsing faster than ever. Those that are still alive are seeking to slash costs and boost profits through more and more deployment of technology.

UBS foresees a rich future—but only for those nations, organizations, and individuals equipped to function in it:

> . . . a range of entirely new companies and
> sectors will spring into existence. For nations,
> the largest gains from the Fourth Industrial
> Revolution are likely to be captured by those
> with the most flexible economies, adding a
> further incentive for governments to trim red
> tape and barriers to business. (Treanor, 2016)

The key to future economic success for nations and individuals alike is flexibility. We agree with UBS on this point. But this is also where the whole vision falls apart. Because we can't even keep up with the pace of tech change today, let alone tomorrow; as anyone familiar with Moore's Law also knows, these changes are only going to accelerate. (Moore's

Law tells us that computing power doubles every two years. And while this is based on observation, rather than being a physical law, it has proved over the last 40 years to hold true.)

Why disruptive tech companies will not solve the jobs crisis

How many Ubers, Googles, Trip Advisors, and Airbnbs does it take to create just a million jobs? Every single one of these "disruptive innovators" (or whatever MBA-style label you wish to put on them) is profitable—at least for a short time. This is because they need very few employees, relative to their revenues and capital. Unlike traditional businesses, their capital is not in human assets, it is in tech assets. Robots are not paid a salary. And they don't go shopping—which supports and grows an economy.

Worse, the traditional industries that they disrupt are "people heavy"—that is, they engage a high number of employees. So this is a double whammy because the job-lite businesses are destroying the job-heavy ones. This is the horrible economic reality of disruptive business models.

Neither UBS nor any other financial contributor, to my knowledge, has any practical remedy for this cannibalization of jobs. One glimmer of hope is that since zero marginal cost means that the daily cost of living will be less, this should help those on a tight household income.

The trouble for national governments is that achieving the necessary labor mobility and flexibility to respond to these disruptions is fraught with difficulty. And even if governments could do this efficiently, making it happen quickly enough is almost impossible when we consider the different speeds at which technology and our people, organizations and institutions are capable of moving.

UBS and other companies will ensure that they do very nicely if their vision or anything close to it actually materializes. Indeed, there will be many more "super rich" in the world. However, there will also be a great many more who used to be comfortable but are now becoming very uncomfortable. This is the future unless we all prepare for it right now.

Summary: Disruptive business models

Smaller, flexible, disruptive companies will undermine larger companies. Although larger companies may seem to have more jobs and seem "safer," disruptive companies can quickly steal market share through the use of automation and technology and a jobs-lite business model. Consequently, we need a process to foresee the vulnerability to our current jobs, the business, and the industry. We also must be able to identify opportunities where our skill sets are needed and valued.

Engine of change No. 4: Education and the speed of institutional change

Our learning systems are rooted deep in the educational institutions and practices of developed nations. Historically, our greatest academic institutions have been considered almost gatekeepers to career opportunities. Yet right now, even education is being disrupted and faces its own crisis as it struggles to respond to employer needs.

One of the greatest ironies of the jobs crisis is that there is actually a *shortage* of the most in-demand technical workers in the world's developed economies. Many employers claim they can't find enough people with the right technical skills. An H-1B visa allows an employer to hire a noncitizen because that individual's skill set is both unique and unavailable from the domestic labor pool. The rising number of H-1B visas issued in the US is frequently cited as evidence that the US. educational institutions are not creating enough skilled workers for the vacant jobs they seek to fill.

So if you are STEM qualified (science, technology, engineering, and math) and you are seeking career opportunities in the US, you might assume that you would have plenty of choices. But chances are you'd be wrong.

How can this be? The fact is simply that *a few* STEM job categories are exploding, while most others are shrinking. The ones that are exploding are growing so fast that they distort the overall picture.

Just for clarity, let's say that many people with highly refined math skills are qualified as quantitative analysts. Unfortunately, technology is taking over many elements of those jobs. So there is no shortage in that sector of the math area. On the other hand, software development is rapidly growing in the areas of biotech and medical technology, robotics, and nanotech. There is so much need that it tips the scales and distorts the need for STEM-trained job candidates.

Here are the facts. Every two years, the US Bureau of Labor Statistics (US-BLS) produces employment projections forecasting job vacancies over the next decade. The latest US-BLS employment projections (for 2012–2022) predict that computing will be the number one most-in-demand STEM skill set for the foreseeable future. In fact, the US-BLS predicts that the three STEM jobs with the most growth will *all* be in computing; only one other area (civil engineering) is expected to generate more than 5000 new jobs per year (US Bureau of Labor Statistics Employment Projections, 2014–24).

By contrast, the US-BLS predicts that each year, there will be over 22,000 new software development jobs, over 12,500 new systems analyst jobs, and over 11,000 new computing support jobs. These statistics also predict significant growth in jobs for computer security, programmers, and network and system administrators.

The data indicates that for the foreseeable future in the US, *nearly 3 out of 4 **new** job openings and 3 out of 5 **total** job openings are going to be in computing.* With all these jobs materializing in the area of computing, it would be great if people could become suitably qualified by taking a course or two to acquire the skills needed. But that is not the case. The basic computer literacy (i.e., knowing Microsoft Word, Excel, or PowerPoint) or CAD-design skills will *not* qualify a person for one of these careers, most of which require advanced computing skills that a person can only gain by fluency and experience in specific computer coding languages. Even general coding knowledge is inadequate for many of these roles, which typically require native application programming skills such as Apple's iOS or Android.

The skills obstacle can be traced back to our educational institutions

With all these unfilled jobs, you'd expect US students would be flocking to computing. Yet recently, the opposite has been true. The Taulbee survey shows that the number of graduates with PhDs in computing has remained at less than 10,000 each year since 2004–2005. (You may be wondering about the "PhD" . . . but keep reading and we will explain.)

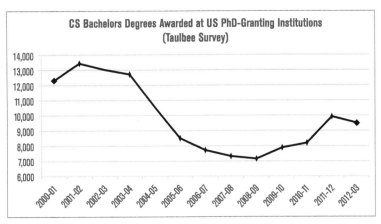

https://cs.calvin.edu/images/department/jobs/2022/05.Taulbee-Bachelors-Degrees-Awarded.png

So the demand for computing-related professionals is exploding, but until recently, fewer US students have been choosing to study the subjects needed for these careers. And while more US students have been studying computer science since 2009, the supply of computer science graduates in the US is still just a fraction of the demand for them.

At this point, you might be thinking, "A PhD in computing! That can't be the requirement! I know some programmers who don't even have a bachelor's degree in *anything!* . . . and they are making a mint. The company that interviewed them gave them a programming project and they were hired!"

Good point! What has been described is a workaround by companies. It's a fairly new development. The reason that we are using the PhD as the standard is simply because it is being used by organizations that are watching the numbers. So please bear with us as we are using the best numbers that we can find to determine what is happening. This will be made clearer in the next chart.

To put this supply-demand imbalance into perspective, the next chart compares the US-BLS Total Jobs projections in the various STEM categories against the most recent National Science Foundation data on the number of bachelor's degrees that were awarded in science and engineering:

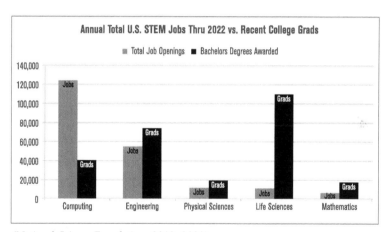

(National Science Foundation, 2012–2022)

We can see here a significant discrepancy between the predicted jobs for mathematics, physical sciences, and engineering. However, with the supply of graduates exceeding the number of job openings, life sciences graduates are massively oversupplied, while computing graduates are in severe shortage. This oversupply means that some of these grads will be unable to find jobs, and oversupply tends to keep salaries flat. (Life science jobs deal with microorganisms, plants, animals, and human beings. These jobs include biology, medicine, or ecology—as well as related considerations like bioethics.)

NOTE: You may recall that we cited jobs in medicine as being some of the least at-risk. That is true if we look solely at the impact of technology. But this doesn't mean that these jobs will be increasing nearly fast enough to absorb the excessive creation of life-sciences graduates.

Companies in need of advanced computing skills are competing hard for the few jobseekers with those skills. By contrast, noncomputing STEM jobseekers are facing stiff competition for the few jobs within their disciplines.

The chart above also explains the confusion in Congress over H-1B visas. Some representatives argue the need for more H-1B visas, while others fiercely refute this. As you can see, the chart shows there is a shortage of workers with advanced computing skills, but there is an oversupply of workers with science, engineering, or mathematics skills. So the confusion in Congress is because one group of representatives are talking about the *T* in STEM, while the other group is talking about the *S*, *E*, and *M* in STEM.

So there's really little to debate about whether there is an undersupply or oversupply of STEM skills. Everything depends on what area of STEM skills we are talking about. Some researchers and commentators continue to use the *aggregate total* number of people holding STEM degrees as their prime metric to measure the total available workforce. And on this basis they wrongly conclude that the supply is ample to meet the needs of employers. As we have explained above, this level of specificity is simply inadequate to explain what is really going on.

While we have focused here only on STEM jobs, this illustrates that our educational institutions are failing to deliver the right mix of skilled workers for employers. This failure means that both employers and workers are being handicapped by a skewed supply-and-demand situation not of their own making.

But there is a further reason why STEM and indeed *any* educational qualifications are not automatically the key to a job. Employers no longer view educational qualifications as their key measure for employment. It's only one factor, and it partially qualifies you for consideration, not for hiring. So it's perfectly accurate for employers to say they have a skills shortage because educational qualifications alone do not make candidates automatically employable. They also require evidence of relevant previous work experience and cultural fit.

While some respected researchers and academics assert that education is key to employability in the 21st century, this is only one part of the picture. In the global jobs crisis, education alone doesn't get people hired. In essence, our educational system and its institutions are not producing enough of the skills that employers want, and they are not changing fast enough.

The disruption of education: the speed of institutional change
As we have already described, the workplace is changing faster than ever before. Skill sets that used to be relevant for ten or even twenty years or more are often now valueless after five years or less. The pace of change in the digital age is so fast that educational institutions are struggling to keep up.

Already cracks are appearing in the higher educational sector. When Corinthian Colleges Inc. was forced in July 2014 to sell off or close nearly all of its 107 campuses, it left 72,000 students with seriously disrupted futures.

For centuries, higher education was bound to physical locations, and thus disruption by others was very difficult. Yet today this barrier is being steadily eroded by the Internet, which enables almost anyone to capture, stream, and distribute content. Today's higher education is responding by placing more courses online and making these available to people around the globe.

But while universities are developing online content, they are not fundamentally disrupting learning because the method of delivery is not a new business model. Professor Clayton Christensen at the Harvard Business School, one of the world's leading authorities on disruptive innovation, says: "Online education is truly going to kill us." And he's a voice from inside the system (Suster, 2013).

Christiansen believes that the most effective way to learn is a sequence where:

1. Learning content is delivered directly to those in the workforce.

2. The workforce can then instantly apply what they're taught.

3. Finally, they immediately report back in the class-room to discuss the implementation.

We think this sort of change seems an obvious response to the skills and learning challenges of the 21st century. But educational institutions are large and unwieldy bureaucracies. Their model is to plan and execute in time units of years—which seems an incredibly archaic idea in today's world. Consequently, our educational institutions are already out of touch, and we have to question what their relevance will be in the coming years and decades.

Again, this bears repeating: the smallest unit of time measurement used in the planning and organization of educational institutions is a year, which is far too slow to keep up with a world being endlessly accelerated by technological advances. Undergraduates spend four years in their programs: freshman, sophomore, junior, and senior . . . each level of classes is one year. Their programs are divided into four levels of challenge and with each year, the sophistication and depth of the courses increases. We differentiate courses as "freshman level" or "It's a senior level course." These time frames cannot possibly keep up with the speed of change from the perspective of business, the economy, and technology.

Summary: Education and the speed of institutional change
Traditional higher education no longer guarantees employability. It's expensive, slow, and too disconnected from the real needs of employers. Students are not able to acquire the skills they need to excel in the 21st century. Worse, a whole generation of young people have taken on huge personal debt to acquire qualifications that frequently have little or no value in the workplace. Even the institutions, whose position and authority seemed unchallengeable, are having to face up to a future which looks more uncertain than at any time in their history.

The challenge for everyone in the coming years will be knowing how to sustain a successful career without reliance on the institutions whose traditional role was to support us in our career goals.

The digital future requires an entirely different set of skills in the workplace for just about anyone who wants to work for a living in the 21st century. People and society must change at a faster pace than ever before to keep from being left behind.

Another point that bears mention concerns the "American Dream." When the baby boomers prepared for college, their parents often encouraged them to "follow their dream." College-bound students were encouraged to pursue a course of study based on their desires and enjoyment. Both parent and young adult believed that there would be a job, a career, and a livelihood waiting for them when they finished college.

Many millennials did exactly that, and when they graduated, they found the world had changed and their degree had no credibility to a potential employer. Even at the writing of this book, many college grads are finding that they have a useless degree that many employers find obsolete.

Engine of change No. 5: Demographics and the aging population

Many middle management executives have aspired to retire comfortably in Florida after decades of hard work. This was once a perfectly reasonable aspiration. However, those days and those hopes have faded and disappeared for most workers over 50.

We all knew the way our careers were supposed to go. Roughly speaking, we'd get a set of good qualifications, start work, change employers maybe four or five times, work hard, get promoted, and then at around 50 or so have a comfortable cruise towards our retirement at 65. We fully expected that we would be able to relax and enjoy the next 20 or so years.

That seems like a fairy tale now for most workers over 50. It doesn't make much difference what your employer or financial advisor recommends. If you are a baby boomer in the US, the UK, or much of the EU, unless you've been so successful (or lucky) in your career that you are sitting on a very large pension fund, this outcome seems about as likely as winning a lottery.

According to a poll by the Associated Press-NORC Center for Public Affairs Research at the University of Chicago, today in the US, some 82 percent of workers aged 50 and older say it is at least "somewhat likely" they will work for pay in retirement. Almost half of boomers polled now expect to retire later than they previously thought—on average nearly three years later than what they thought at age 40.

People have a habit of being unduly optimistic when thinking about their financial position if it's much beyond the next year or so. This is due to a combination of denial and difficulty in facing up to harsh realities. When our focus is on surviving month by month, planning for the next 20 or 30 years is a luxury fewer and fewer people can indulge in.

The impact of more and more older workers, who simply cannot afford to retire from the overall workforce, has massive implications for a society already struggling to adapt to the changes we have outlined. Older workers with few current technology skills will be competing for low paid jobs along with younger graduates with the wrong qualifications. This keeps pay low and opportunities scarce for both groups.

If this scenario sounds unduly pessimistic, there is plenty of data to support it. Some of the statistics emerging in the US are really horrific. One in six baby boomers reported having less than $1,000 in retirement savings, and one in four indicated that they aren't saving for retirement outside of Social Security. Some 12 percent of non-retired people reported borrowing from a 401(k) or other retirement plan in the past year. Though 29 percent reported at least $100,000 in savings, some find even that's not nearly enough.

"All too often, people have a lump-sum illusion. They think, 'I have $100,000 in my 401(k),' then they think, 'I'm rich,'" said Olivia Mitchell, a retirement specialist who teaches at the University of Pennsylvania. "But it doesn't add up to much. It certainly is not going to keep them in champagne and truffles" (Sedensky, 2013).

If you are thinking that this is a blip or a phase, that would be a mistake. This is a destruction of the life expectations of an entire generation. The traditional career ladder has disappeared. At the bottom, our educational institutions are pumping out ever more educated young people into the jobs market. At the other end, older workers with inadequate funds to even consider retirement are desperately seeking ways to extend their earning ability. In the middle are employees with ever growing workloads as they are being asked to do the work of two or even three people.

According to the National Center for Health Statistics, the millennial generation is the largest generation to enter the workforce in the history of the United States. The following shows generational years and births (Gronback, 2008):

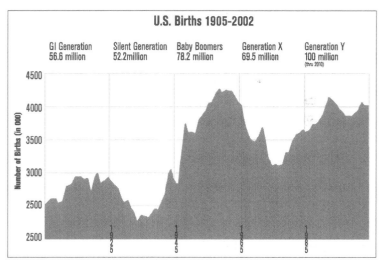

Gronbach, Kenneth W. (2008). The Age Curve: How to Profit from the Coming Demographic Storm *(p.9). Retrieved from https://books.google.com/ books/about/The_Age_Curve.html?id=rNAG_9IQ4loC&printsec=frontcover&s ource=kp_read_button&hl=en#v=onepage&q&f=false*

Births from
- 1925–1945: 52.5 million (silent generation)
- 1945–1965: 78.2 million (baby boomers)
- 1965–1985: 69.5 million (Generation X)
- 1985–2010: 100 million (Generation Y "millennials")

A normal distribution of wealth would look like a diamond. There would be a few rich at the top, a few poor at the bottom and the "middle" class in the middle. Today, many people see that the middle class is shrinking and pushed lower, creating a pyramid.

This book is, to a certain extent, about income mobility—the ability to move higher in income, which increases quality of life. At the top of the wealth distribution are the super-wealthy; then come millions of older workers who are seeking ways to sustain their earnings. Then come a growing class of underemployed (yet more educated than ever) early career people. They are unable to find work that enables them to gain the experience they need to start their careers. A few in the middle are doing okay, but they too must resist forces thrusting them downward to the over-crowded bottom of the pyramid.

This last group, as indicated by the numbers, are the largest demographic. The point is that there has to be a way to get out of the lower group and onto the stairs where even small changes will make a huge difference in the quality of one's living situation. The six engines of change block the staircase and compress the corridor.

Meanwhile, employers report ever-increasing difficulties in finding the skills they seek. Naturally, they want people with specific experience in the work they require to be done. But there is a problem: as work transforms in the digital age, older people don't have experience with the current technologies, and younger people don't have the proven track record of accomplishments.

We have an impasse. On the one hand, job vacancies grow and grow; on the other hand, greater numbers of people are looking for work and are unable to find it. We cannot change these conditions. What we can change is how we manage our careers and behave in a world of work unlike any that has ever existed before. It is the goal of this book to help you navigate this scenario.

Engine of change No. 6: Fiscal policy

As of 2016, the United States remains stuck in a paralyzed economy eight years after the onset of the 2008 recession.

The Obama Administration and the Federal Reserve have spent more on government-based economic stimulus than at any other time in America's history, with little to show for the trillions of dollars spent.

At around 2.2 percent annual growth, we are witnessing the slowest "recovery" in history. According to the Council on Foreign Relations, "the economic expansion following the 2008 recession has been the weakest of the post–World War II era" (Walker, 2013).

And as anyone who follows economic cycles knows, the gap between recessions is on average five to ten years. The US is currently due for another recession even before we have recovered from the last one:

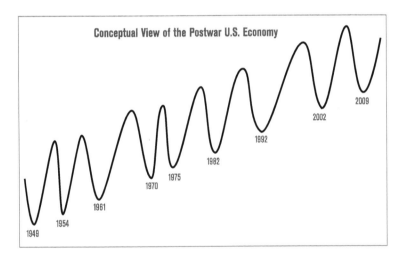

Conceptual View of the Postwar U.S. Economy

Andrew Huszar of Rutgers Business School wrote in *The Wall Street Journal* that "the Fed may have created and spent over $4 trillion for a total return of as little as 0.25% of GDP (i.e., a mere $40 billion bump in U.S. economic output). Both of those estimates indicate that QE (quantitative easing) isn't really working" (Huszar, 2013). *http://www.wsj.com/articles/ SB10001424052702303763804579183680751473884*

The traditional levers of economic policy for governments—i.e., low interest rates, quantitative easing, and investment in federal programs such as the Affordable Care Act (Obamacare)—have failed to ignite economic growth and hence job creation in the US following the Great Recession of 2008.

The jobs crisis isn't going to get better overnight. Regardless of who wins the election, a new president cannot fix this problem. Earlier in the history of the United States, a president could have a clear impact on jobs through changes in business taxation and policies that encouraged businesses to hire. Today, the changes we have described in this book take the problem out of the hands of government.

The postindustrial world is one in which the United States' principal strengths in natural resources and manufacturing capacity have been diminished by the rise of other countries matching or exceeding this ability to manufacture their way to global dominance.

American firms like Apple might be among the most envied in the world, but they have abdicated any responsibility to support jobs at home. American business is suffering a crisis of confidence, which depresses investment. The tax burdens that attempt to diminish the explosion of government debt since 2008 are unsurprisingly strangling business expansion at home.

Obama and his successor have an impossible conundrum to solve. It's natural that the president wants a more equitable society in the US, as well as a growing economy. But the big levers the government can pull are limited. Higher taxation can redistribute wealth and slow the growth of government debt, but in the process, it kills domestic business confidence, investment, and jobs.

Thousands of new regulations flowing from the Obama Administration every year have strangled economic growth and discouraged investment. James Gattuso and Diane Katz wrote that Obama-era regulations " . . . are not just a problem for entrepreneurs. American workers and their families have been hit hard by the persistent lack of job creation that results, in part, from regulatory excesses" (Gattuso, 2012).

Summary: Fiscal policy

It doesn't matter what we think of the US leadership, the influencers have changed. Many other countries are in this same situation. This isn't an exclusively US problem, it's a global one. For the first time in history, the traditional levers of government economic policy are virtually powerless to address these destructive economic challenges.

In this situation, all people can do is try to protect themselves in a world where nothing can be taken for granted. Regardless of whose fault it is, the reality is that the world can never return to anything remotely resembling the great American Dream. The best option is to figure out our own survival plan. If neither business nor government can be relied upon to help us, we have to take care of ourselves.

Lessons learned: Eight economic consequences

This book up to now may have been somewhat dismal. However, we hope that you will also have found it fascinating. We hope that you now have greater insight into the global economic picture. At the very least, we hope that, at this point, you have a greater understanding and appreciation of the interconnectivity of geopolitics, business, economics, education, demographics, and technology and how they impact our job prospects.

Although some of this section is review, it will bring a synopsis of the current situation. This is where it gets exciting, because now that we know where we are, we can put together a plan to successfully manage our future.

Consequence No. 1: Jobs, business, and the digital age

No serious discussion about jobs and work can really take place without considering organizational behavior, the business climate, and the political environment. It's tempting to hope that as the US and the UK crawl out of their recession, the economy will be on the path to recovery, and all will eventually be well. In the Eurozone (those European nations that use the euro as their currency), most members are coping, and a few are even beginning to recover.

The trouble is that the recession is actually something of a red herring. Its aftermath, in terms of job losses, makes it tempting to assume that the recession alone was what caused so many job losses. If we accept this idea, then an economic recovery, however fragile, must be good news for jobs.

Well, it is and it isn't. The trouble is that the recession has actually masked what's been going on at a structural level in the job market. Behind the headlines of the recession and its fallout, there is a much less visible transformation of jobs and the world of work that is rarely discussed.

So what is at the root of this restructuring if it's not the recession? It's technology.

Here's a quick review: As we discussed earlier (Engine of Change No. 2), technology is a double-edged sword. On the one hand, we love how it empowers us to do more things faster, more easily, and less expensively than ever before. These are good reasons to appreciate technology. On the other hand, technology is destroying jobs faster than the economy can replace them.

It's also having a profound and often counterproductive impact on the hiring processes used by organizations. One quick example is the applicant tracking systems (ATS) that have been developed for the hiring industry to screen applicants before submitting them to a human resources department. We'll get into this in detail later in the book when we discuss cover letters and résumés.

Those who warn that technological advancements are a threat are usually labeled Luddites and cast into the doghouse. We are not making a Luddite argument, however. We accept that technological progress is a generally a good thing. What we are presenting is the idea that the impact of technology today is so profound, widespread, and rapid that even the most highly skilled and professional people must closely monitor these advancements to sustain a rewarding career in the coming years and decades.

Consequence No. 2: The replacement of high-paid jobs by low-paid jobs

The jobs that are returning post-recession are not the same as the ones lost.

We are certain that middle-class jobs have been destroyed in the wake of the 2007–2008 financial collapse. The growth in new jobs reported gleefully by US and UK governments have been almost entirely low-wage and part-time jobs. And there is little reason to believe this situation can be quickly or easily reversed.

A recent presentation from the Federal Reserve Bank of San Francisco describes the jobs "recovery" in stark terms. The vast majority of job losses during the recession were in middle-income occupations, and they've largely been replaced by low-wage jobs since 2010 (Federal Reserve Bank of San Francisco, 2013).

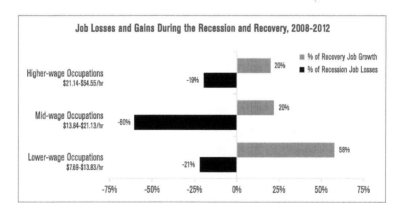

Mid-wage occupations made up a staggering 60 percent of the job losses during the recession. But mid-wage jobs represent just 22 percent of the jobs gained during the recovery.

By contrast, low-wage occupations have totally dominated the recovery. They represent 58 percent of the job gains since 2010. According to the San Francisco Fed, "Many middle-class workers have lost their jobs and, if they have been able to secure new employment at all, find themselves earning far lower wages post-recession" (Plumer, 2013).

Nearly 40 percent of the jobs gained since the recovery began—about 1.7 million—have come from three low-wage sectors: food services, retail, and employment services.

According to the Bureau of Labor Statistics (US-BLS), four low-wage occupations are now the top four types of

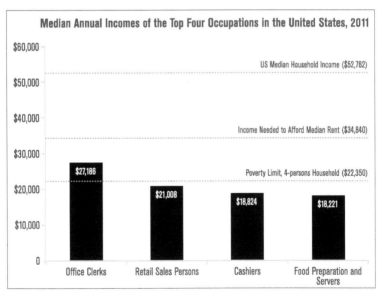

(Bureau of Labor Statistics Occupational Employment and Wage Estimates, 2011)

employment in the US: retail salespeople, cashiers, office clerks, and food preparers and servers:

This problem of low wages is compounded by the fact that industries that employ mid-wage earners, such as construction, manufacturing, insurance, real estate and IT, have either stagnated or grown too slowly to recover their pre-recession losses. Additionally, budget cuts to federal and state government have eliminated a vast swathe of mid- and higher-wage government jobs. And a separate chunk of middle-wage jobs including carpenters, plumbers, plasterers and electricians are still waiting for the U.S. housing market to recover.

Consequence No. 3: The growth of wealth inequality

The distribution of wealth among the population is widening for several reasons.

1. *Workforce polarization:* Over the past decade, both high and low-wage jobs have been growing. But jobs in the middle continue to shrink. Mid-wage jobs suffered a major drop after 2001, largely stagnated during the 2000s, and have now declined even further in the most recent downturn.

2. *New technologies:* Economists have been debating the causes of this divergence between high and low paying jobs. Harvard's Lawrence Katz and Claudia Goldin argue that new technologies and machines are now displacing mid-wage jobs (Plumer, 2013).

   We believe this is a correct analysis. But it's not the full story.

Some others, such as Larry Mishel of the Economic Policy Institute, point to political factors, from the decline of labor unions to trade liberalization to the dwindling minimum wage. This is a factor too, but again it's only an ingredient in the mix, not the full disastrous recipe (Mischel, 2012).

3. *Government debt:* Neither of these arguments discusses the lead weight pulling the whole economy down. And that weight is government debt, which puts massive upward pressure on tax and limits government spending—the type of spending that would create more jobs in the public sector.

It seems logical that there's no single, simple explanation of what's going on. It's multi-faceted, which makes it complex to understand and remedy both at a national and individual level.

But if the debt trend continues, it will amplify something which is already a big problem in the western economies: income inequality. And with it comes the destruction of the hopes and aspirations of the largest part of society—the middle class.

Consequence No. 4: The separation of GDP growth and household incomes

For the first time in US history, economic growth is no longer driving income improvements at the household level.

Traditionally, improvements in GDP have directly resulted in increased income and prosperity for citizens. In the US, this link has broken. US median household income is now at a lower level than it was in 1999. As we saw in the last chapter, even though US GDP has been on the rise since 2009, household income has been falling since 2008. As technology continues to increase productivity and reduces marginal costs, we have GDP growth but no wealth creation except for those who are in the boardrooms and/or those that have major investments in the stocks and bond markets, i.e., those who own liquid financial assets.

To look at it in its simplest terms, businesses can increase their profits with fewer employees. Jeremey Rifkin's book, *The Third Industrial Revolution*, described this evolution elegantly. Rifkin reminds us how the first industrial revolution substituted human muscle power with mechanical devices. The second industrial revolution transformed transport and communications. And the third industrial revolution is replacing human cognitive tasks with artificial intelligence.

Until recently, technological improvements have only really affected those who sold their manual labor to earn a living. Today's technology is reducing the workforce needed for tasks that also required the application of professional and mental skills.

But jobs requiring the application of skill and knowledge are different from jobs where we simply provide our time and manual labor. The acquisition of knowledge-based skills and competencies can take years, sometime decades. And if no one wants those skills anymore, jobseekers will have a stark choice: either face another layoff and start again or try to compete for low-paying work.

The American middle class has skills that fewer and fewer people want or need to pay for. Educational institutions are not helping supply the skills we need either. So gaining the deep skills needed for software development requires years of experience. Using a computer is different from developing the software. Latter-career jobseekers don't have the time to acquire such deep skills even though they may have the skills to use the software.

This is the reality of the polarization of the West's workforce: greater wealth acquisition by those at the top (those who own assets) but falling income levels for everyone else—not just the poorest but the vast majority of people, those that politicians like to describe as "hardworking families."

Consequence No. 5: Government debt constrains its ability to stimulate jobs growth

The US national debt is projected to swell to 100 percent of the economy by 2038, due primarily to the enormous cost of caring for an aging society. This may seem of no consequence to you. But it defines the future fiscal and economic landscape for all Americans regardless of who is in the White House. Whether Democrats or Republicans hold sway, for the rest of our lives government debt will hang over us all, constraining policy options and creating additional tax burdens on citizens for decades to come.

As we described earlier, excessive debt limits the choices available to any individual, organization, or government that holds it. The consequence of growing US government debt for employment is that the government simply cannot afford to intervene in a significant way to create jobs. And in any case, governments have traditionally had a poor record of job creation.

Because US government debts continue to grow unchecked, these debts will continue to be passed to individual citizens directly and indirectly through the giant levers of fiscal policy.

Three points define the current situation:

- US government debt acts as a brake on government's ability to seize the initiative in the area of job creation.

- US government debt means the tax outlook for citizens will not significantly improve anytime soon.

- Monetary realities always override policy ideals, so future political and policy changes to stimulate job creation are not likely be of value to many people.

The only sensible conclusion is that we all need to come up with our own personal solution. We need to become our own personal economists and marketers and take control of our own career initiatives. And we intend that the latter part of this book will help you do just that.

Consequence No. 6: Economic recovery won't bring back jobs

If we have any future recovery in the economy that delivers greater GDP and business profits, this is unlikely to translate to significantly increased household wealth or many more jobs. That's because increased business profits will be reinvested not in people but in technology.

Businesses and employers view people not as an asset (despite their frequent protestations to the contrary). They view them as a cost and a management challenge. Machines do not take vacations. They do not complain. They do not need supervision or management. They do not ask for a raise. What business owner is going to choose to invest any more of their profits in people than the absolute minimum they need to?

So we all need to think differently about our jobs and careers in the 21st century. This isn't something talked about in the mainstream media as they generally report job losses and stories about new jobs being created. At best, you'll find tips about interviews or résumé writing. However, interview skills and a better-written résumé will not help you deal with these fundamental changes in society, which will become more and more dominant in the future.

Our personal survival plan needs therefore to be based not on any hope for significant economic recovery but on a clear understanding that the world has changed forever. We all need to have a plan that reflects this new world rather than simply seeking to extend our survival in the old one.

Consequence No. 7: The impact of the Zero Marginal Cost Society

Jeremy Rifkin's book, *The Zero Marginal Cost Society* has set out an immensely insightful view of what's really going on. As Rifkin says, "We are just beginning to glimpse the bare outlines of an emerging new economic system, the collaborative commons. This is the first new economic paradigm to emerge on the world scene since the advent of capitalism and socialism in the early 19th century. So it's a remarkable historical event. It has long-term implications for society."

Rifkin's view is that technology will make goods and services ever cheaper until they are almost free. The trigger for this global change is something called "zero marginal cost." Marginal costs are the costs of producing an extra unit of a good or service after your fixed costs are covered.

We can see examples of ever-falling marginal costs everywhere in our day-to-day lives. Marginal costs have been falling consistently for decades as technology progressively replaced expensive human labor and drove down the cost of production. I distinctly recall wanting a flat-screen television about twelve years ago. I never bought one then, because they cost about $10,000. Last year I could (and did) buy a bigger and much better TV for less than $1000. Today I could buy an even better one for probably about $600.

Endlessly falling marginal cost means consumer goods and many services will continue to get cheaper and cheaper, heading ever closer to zero. Zero or near-zero marginal cost will soon dramatically affect every single person in the world in every aspect of their lives.

3D printing, today in its infancy, will soon transform how goods are made, sold, and acquired. But it won't be a simple transfer of manufacturing wealth from old firms to new ones. Not only will the market for big firms be reduced by elimination of retail intermediaries, intensified competition, shorter life cycles, and Internet disintermediation (the delivery of almost-free products and services direct from the supplier to the consumer); these trends will replace markets with even bigger but much less profitable ones. We've already seen more than enough evidence of this process as it destroyed and fragmented the music, publishing, and news empires that once ruled the world.

Zero or near-zero marginal cost will transform jobs. For example, the cost of sending e-mails and searching the Internet was initially expensive as businesses were charged by the data that was uploaded or downloaded. Many of those costs have been reduced through cloud computing and other online technologies. In a similar way, the zero marginal cost will also transform our personal costs of living. We will simply need to spend less to enjoy a similar standard of living because the things we consume will continue to become ever cheaper.

This is good news! Even if your income is static, your standard of living may get better as certain goods and services become less expensive. This is a macroeconomic view. Jobseekers or employees should track the cost of goods and services that are currently moving toward the zero marginal cost society. Which are getting less expensive? If the jobseeker is in a sector with falling consumer prices, watch out.

It's important to realize that not everything is headed in this direction. But many things will.

Consequence No. 8: Death by a thousand cuts for large employers

When we look at who's hiring and who's firing, we see a pattern. Generally, large employers are downsizing and laying people off. Their businesses are being eroded at the edges by smaller, faster-moving competitors—the disruptive businesses that investors and the media get so excited about.

Job creation is typically happening within smaller businesses. They are responding to the way technology is enabling them to set up and grow faster and more cheaply than ever before. But while their innovation and enterprise are good things, they have hidden consequences for the workforce.

Two changes are causing a reduction in the number of jobs within 21st century businesses:

1. They need fewer people.
2. They require different skills.

Change No. 1: 21st century businesses employ fewer people

Let's consider an example. I just looked at TripAdvisor's page for hotels in Rome. There were 1.6 million reviews posted for that city alone. How much would it cost and how long would it take to compile that many reviews the old-fashioned way? Certainly far more time and money than TripAdvisor spent on creating the software to allow its users to post them for free.

TripAdvisor can keep their overheads low and even make use of "work" that they acquire completely free. TripAdvisor and many other online businesses use members' feedback instead of their own work to create much of their online content and value. Business models such as this keep the firm's headcount to an absolute minimum.

Some argue that these new disruptive business models are a good thing: they smash through older, more expensive, and less innovative business models to create a whole new way of serving the customer. And this model drives change for the better. That's a fine argument from the point of view of technology, business, and consumers. But it's not so fine when we look at jobs.

As of December 2014, TripAdvisor employed a total of 2,793 people. But how many jobs has TripAdvisor eliminated in the travel industry? It's probably fair to say that more than a few travel writers and hotel inspectors have suddenly found themselves with a lot less work. But the disruptive nature of TripAdvisor means that suddenly a vast swath of the hotel and travel agency industry has found itself shrinking or even obsolete as consumers abandon costly services in favor of self-service and ultimately purchase through TripAdvisor and its affiliates/advertisers.

Even in 2012, according to Mintel, seven in ten people who took a holiday booked entirely online. Fewer than one in ten customers now believe that travel agents are better informed about holiday destinations than review websites such as TripAdvisor.

Change No. 2: The newly available jobs require different skills

Disruptive businesses like TripAdvisor require skills different from those employed at the businesses they are leapfrogging (i.e., bypassing them and stealing their market).

Let's say you are a mid-ranking database manager in a large organization. You spend a good deal of your time participating in the day-to-day management of the business. If your employer's business has been disrupted by the sort of change that is caused by Trip Advisor and your job is eliminated, then you need to find another one fast. What do you, as an employee, actually have that is of value to another employer that you have acquired from your now extinct job?

You know about your sector and how your previous employer managed the business. Is that enough to get you rehired? Increasingly the answer to that question is simply no. You do not possess enough value or relevant knowledge for another employer. And if you are in a disrupted sector, the job vacancies that mirrored your last job responsibilities are not going to be there anyway.

This is the hard reality of disruptive businesses and their impact on jobs. Simply switching employers is becoming a less and less reliable way of securing a future income.

Four essential career concepts

All this rapid change has meant that jobs have become scarcer for more and more people. Even where human skills are required to deliver services, like healthcare and the arts, the ever-increasing efficiency of the technology used to empower these activities means fewer and fewer people are needed.

The implications of the zero marginal cost society are huge. We all need to think differently about how we will earn a living in the coming years. There are several implications:

1. Even if we are currently working full-time, it is almost certain that the number of people that organizations require to do the type of work we do will continue to diminish.

2. As traditional jobs continue to become scarcer, competition for the remaining jobs will continue to become fiercer.

3. The loss of a job is likely to result in longer periods without work. The loss of income coupled with continuing living expenses will continue to bankrupt many people.

Placing our entire faith in our skills and qualifications that have supported our careers until now will no longer guarantee our income in the future. We all need to plan for this eventuality, and the starting point for this planning is how we assess the personal value we bring to a potential employer. This may entail much different competencies from the ones that have enabled our careers in the past.

We believe that we can keep ahead of this tsunami of job destruction if we embrace four essential ideas about our careers in the Internet age:

Concept No. 1: The long-term view

Most people think about their lives in one-year timelines. The speed at which we are experiencing change is accelerating faster than our thinking. We are traveling faster than ever before, and we have to look ahead of the curve to stay on track.

Concept No. 2: Connectivity–Your personal network

The Internet facilitates the development of our personal networks. The largest numbers of opportunities will accrue to those who are the best-connected people. This is why LinkedIn and other social media are so important to all of us.

Concept No. 3: Collaboration rather than competition

Collaborative approaches will yield greater returns than competitive ones. Building our opportunities will be less and less the result of competition. More and more they will be the result of collaborations. People do business with people they like. And helping others is the best way we know to develop the necessary goodwill for a relationship which has future value to both parties.

Concept No. 4: Intellectual capital and creativity

Personal intellectual capital and especially forms of creativity that cannot be replicated by technology will be the most resistant to job elimination. We tend to think of intellectual capital as a corporate matter. But every one of us has personal intellectual capital that is ours and ours alone. It might be great recipes, a gift for public speaking, or the ability to show great empathy. The list is endless.

More than ever before, we need to understand clearly the value of our personal intellectual and social networks. This will be the only way we can figure out how to leverage our value and continue to earn money in a zero marginal cost society.

The advantage is ours

What this all amounts to is a far cry from the traditional job hunting that most people are familiar with. We'll discuss in due course why job hunting doesn't work anymore. For now, let's just register that the days of job hunting are numbered. The future belongs to those who have and relentlessly pursue a career management strategy. The following sections of this book will provide you with the tools to do just that.

So believe it or not, this can all be used to your advantage. The people who are aware of the relationship between the economy and the jobs market are those who will find a way to manage their careers and provide for their families and their future.

Later in this book, we will help you consider what kinds of skills you should acquire to enhance your career prospects. We will show you how to think differently about your worth to potential employers and how you can control your future and make the world a better place in the process.

PART TWO

CAREER MANAGEMENT

Introduction to career strategy

A successful, fail-safe process to manage your career is critical. It's the foundation of your future success. The process should be dynamic and repeatable—so you can regularly check your current situation against a long-term plan, manage any risks, and adjust course as needed. This is your Career Plan.

> ► Change is constant. It always has been, but the rate of change today is faster than at any other time in human history. This faster rate of change now mandates that we must continuously monitor our situation with intentionality. If we forget, if we let even six months go by without monitoring our income-generation situation, then we could easily be out of a job.

Smart jobseekers must have a working, adaptable plan in place to manage their situation and the path to ensure their future. So as soon as change becomes evident within a company team or unit, the company at large, the industry, or the economy; these astute people already have a plan in place to ensure consistent income.

This includes tracking the CEO and C-Suite, as well as watching your industry for disruptive innovations, and finally keeping an eye on advancements in technology—the application of which will inevitably impact your current situation and provide opportunities that may give you an advantage—*if* you are ready to take advantage of them.

Is this for you? Then . . .

Since your strategy must be updated to track and manage your future, it will entail a life cycle. In other words, you need a process that you can revisit repeatedly that guides you as you track changes in your career, company, and industry. It is a process that you should routinely refer to, update, and adjust so that your career is securely managed and your personal revenue is ensured.

Perhaps you've been on a jobsearch prior to reading this book. From the time that you were laid off, how much time did it take for you to begin your jobsearch? Perhaps you dove right in. You quickly updated an earlier résumé, contacted everyone you could think of and began to apply for jobs. After several weeks and even months, you found that your response rate was nil. Nothing happened. You were no closer to finding a job than you were when you started your search.

Or perhaps you took time to get your bearings and budget your finances as well as your time. Perhaps there was a redistribution of household activities to accommodate the changes in your schedule. Then you began your jobsearch, putting together a résumé and starting or updating your LinkedIn profile. Maybe you visited some jobseeker support groups. Regardless, you were putting together the infrastructure needed to begin a jobsearch.

How long did all that take? Likely, it took a few months. Regardless of the approach, it takes time to get organized.

> ► Since change will be constant, and since your jobsearch will be interrupted by bouts of employment, it is critical to be ready *before* your current position is at risk. To effectively manage your career, you need to have the right tools in place as the foundation of your jobsearch.

Once you have established your foundation, you will be agile, flexible, and ahead of your competition.

Again, we are asking you to consider managing your career through a life cycle—a process of continuous change. Therefore, the process we are about to outline will not stop because you start a new job.

Is this for you? Then . . .

Career design

How many people do you know who work in a toxic environment? How many times have you tried to work in toxic environments? Many jobseekers will forgo pay for a better work atmosphere rather than put up with the stress and angst that come with a toxic workplace.

The big surprise comes when we realize that what is a perfect match for some people may be highly challenging for others—even to the point of becoming untenable. So why does that happen?

Here's a demonstration of the point with a few examples. The point is that the same environment is toxic to some people and not to others.

Example 1: Some people enjoy knowing exactly what is needed, when, and how, and they seek a place where every detail is clear and concise. Yet others, in that same environment, may feel micromanaged. The workplace may feel suffocating. They simply can't work well when they are micromanaged.

Example 2: Many people will tell you that they aren't "idea" people. They can take an idea, bring substance to it, implement it, and along the way, they will improve it! Yet other people are indeed "idea" people, and if their ideas are minimized or if someone takes an idea and doesn't credit them for it—that's unacceptable.

Example 3: Some people thrive on community and team engagement: the more meetings, the better! Others thrive when working alone—a place where they can manage and control the quality of the outcome. These people know about every aspect of their responsibilities, and they carefully monitor them to ensure continuous quality outputs. If there is a problem, they know it is theirs to manage. However, many people need a combination of the two with an ideal balance between them of, say, 40 percent meetings and collaboration and 60 percent working independently or with a small team to get the work done.

The ratio of work that involves collaboration and working independently can change depending on the type of work and from person to person. Either way, ideal situations are specific to the individual. When changes in the work environment alter the balance, a work environment may become toxic. When that happens to a manager, it is not unusual for the entire cadre of direct reports to feel a change in tension.

> ► Understanding the characteristics of a "good" job is your responsibility. If you want a good work environment for yourself, then you are the person to bring definition to what that means. No one else can do this for you.

Further, if you don't do this, others, especially your management, will do it for you. They will choose the parts of your abilities that best suit their needs and assign work to you. They will decide your assignments and the conditions under which you will work—and it is highly unlikely that you will agree with their decisions. Consequently, it is your responsibility to understand the characteristics of your optimum situation, *and* it is your responsibility to educate management in such a way that they *want* to create situations that are as close to your ideal as possible.

When these factors change for the worse—due to new assignments, organizational changes, mergers and acquisitions, and so forth—then you will need to engage your career design plan to identify new opportunities. These opportunities may be right in your current environment or they may be within your business. They may be in another company.

The point here is that by understanding your definition of a good job and the manner in which you bring value, you can be proactive and stay ahead of the unemployment curve and maintain a personal income stream. That's what this section of the book is about.

Case studies: Careers without plans and lessons learned

Marcia: When I moved from the academic and nonprofit worlds into the corporate sector, I often asked people if they enjoyed their job and their career. Most often the answer was a resounding "No!" Sometimes a response would be introspective as the person looked at the floor. Generally, I would invite these people to lunch and ask additional questions.

After well over a hundred lunch conversations over a period of eight years, it became evident that almost every career path shared one common element. Essentially, these people had not managed their career at all. Instead, they had let others do it for them.

When asked for a summary of their career and how each job change happened, their stories were remarkably similar. They would report something like this:

> "My first job was at _____. It was [somewhat boring, marginally interesting] work.

I was diligent and showed up consistently. Bit by bit I learned my way around, and additional responsibilities were delegated to me. After [6 months to 2 years] someone told me about an opening that they thought I could fill. So I applied, and I got the job!

"I did that for a few years and learned a great deal. It was nice to have more interesting work! After two or three years, the same thing happened. Someone who knew me was promoted and needed some [low-cost, early-career] help and asked me to apply for a position that reported to them. I did, and I was hired into that position, which I held for about [5 to 7] years.

"That person left the company and suggested that a new colleague consider me for an opening. I was asked to apply, and that job came through too. So I switched companies."

. . . and the sequence kept repeating itself. Notice that this individual had not proactively sought opportunities that specifically reflected his or her interests. With almost every person I spoke to, no one had any idea of a career goal or a plan to get there. Most everyone had let others make decisions about the next steps in their careers, and they were based on the needs of the people around those making the decisions. Those I spoke with were being used to fill the needs of people who knew them but with no regard for the creation of a fulfilling career—simply because a plan, with specific goals, did not exist. They had no career direction. With very little variation, these people did not like where they ended up, and they felt stuck!

The millennial generation, also known as Gen Y, are those individuals who were born between 1985 and 2010. At the writing of this book, this generation, also known as "Generation Jobless," has a significantly higher unemployment rate compared to mid-career and late career workers, and they have the lowest workforce participation rate of any demographic. Some sources have quoted a 54 percent combined unemployment and underemployment rate for the struggling demographic.

Many of these early career individuals entered college believing that they could pursue their "passion" in college and that after graduation they would find a job that would be fulfilling and satisfying and would meet their financial needs. But the world and the promises of the past changed and they graduated into a harsh world with little patience for their idealism, their dependence on technology, and their seeming lack of patience with large corporate structure. Some entered college and completed a degree that had become obsolete by the time they graduated.

I side with the millennials. They bear the brunt of a terrible "bait and switch." They were repeatedly told to follow their passions, and when they graduated college, the hopes for employment in those career-paths were gone.

The millennial generation sees how corporate and large organizations as well as nonprofit and academic institutions have treated their parents after decades of service. This new generation seeks careers that are meaningful. They want to make the world a better place, and they look for organizations that are socially sensitive and environmentally astute.

While I worked at a large global insurance company, I was part of a team that designed a survey to be given to the early-career employees (who were millennials). The results of the survey indicated that these early-career professionals did not intend to spend more than four years at the company. They were there to learn everything they could to advance their careers and move on. They did not believe the employer had any commitment to their career growth. They were there to do their jobs, and that was it.

How to design a career plan

The first step is to recognize that we are in a new era and consequently, we need to think differently about careers. It is no longer about life satisfaction and the belief that if we are engaged in our passion, then the money will come. This may sound harsh. However, I repeatedly see where the "American Dream" has become a nightmare in terms of generating an income.

It is certainly possible that for some people, engagement with their passion may bring in an income stream. But for most of us, the reality bears out that this is no longer true when it comes to career aspirations. It does not mean that life will have no satisfaction. It means that *career* is now defined as earning a reasonable income—which brings peace of mind! A job that fits should also be satisfying and sustainable.

Career groundwork
New thinking about career definition

As you read the first part of this book, you surely realize that this is no longer about passion-engagement. It is about finding and maintaining a career that is satisfying and sustainable and meets your financial needs.

A word about "passion" in the workplace. Sometimes our "passion" simply cannot be sustained with integrity and with the consistent output that employment demands. Here is a personal example: I love German chocolate cake, especially with a cup of black coffee—but I eat it only once a year, sometimes less often. It is not a sustainable activity. The same goes for many of our passions. Just because we enjoy them doesn't mean that we can sustainably engage with them. (Truthfully, I don't remember when I last had a piece of German chocolate cake.)

A person may love being outdoors, long hiking and camping. They may have a passion for forestry and associated outdoor work. But that doesn't mean there is a market for it. And it doesn't mean that it will pay a consistent income. Further, the job may be wonderful in spring and summer, but when the temperature is well below freezing and the job requires extended periods in cold and wet environments, then the job may lose some of its glamor.

This same principal goes for most seasonal employment. Opportunities in the Parks and Recreation Department, tourism, and the like may not be available year-round. So these positions do not bring in a consistent income.

Likewise, a person may have a passion for crafting and creating unique jewelry. Unless he or she is one of a very few world-class jewelry designers, it is unlikely that this passion will bring in a consistent income. Certainly, if these people have an entrepreneurial spirit *and* a lot of business savvy, then a small business may be an option depending on market demand for their product and their ability to market their expertise.

Satisfying, sustainable, and financially manageable

We believe that a job should have three characteristics. It should be:

- Satisfying
- Sustainable
- Financially manageable

Satisfying means that there is purpose and meaningfulness in the work that you engage in each day while working. *Sustainable* means that you can perform those activities at work every week; week after week, without getting burned out or bored. *Financially manageable* means that the income from the job will meet your needs, hopefully with enough left over for an emergency cushion.

Thinking differently

Career management is about defining a process to ensure a consistent income. Changes in technology and global commerce as well as how hiring is conducted have brought about a need to think differently.

Most people get a job, and then they do that job. It makes sense. Because they have a job, they don't need to be looking for another job, and a company might not appreciate employees who are looking for other opportunities. It seems that such an employee may have a divided mind-set and be a "flight-risk."

Regardless of your situation, the jobs market rarely uses the "gold-watch" model, in which employees begin their career in a company and remain there for the duration of their career. Then they retire and receive a gold watch for their many decades of service. Companies no longer hire someone in their early twenties and expect that individual to spend thirty or forty years with the company.

Actually, the current thinking on the average length of a job assignment is three to four years. These changes may be within one company; however, with the increase of mergers and acquisitions, and the number of disruptions caused by new technology and other factors, it is less and less likely that employees will remain with the same company for multiple stages of their career.

Another factor to consider is that change is happening so quickly that companies can no longer take the time to retrain current employees. Instead, many companies assess their future needs, hire the "already-trained" skills, and lay off people who are no longer needed. Some companies expect employees to develop new skills on their own time and at their own expense.

Reasons for these changes include the globalization of commerce and the rate of change in technology that were discussed earlier in this book. Again, the needs and core competencies needed to sustain a business must be flexible to accommodate their market. So some skill sets will no longer be needed.

This phenomenon is what mandates a change in our thinking about employment. The key factors:

- Changes in technology
- Global business expansion and competition
- Product adaptation for emerging and changing markets
- Disruptive innovations
- Capital transfers from people to AI and robotics
- Decentralization of organizations
- Matrix structures
- The rise of "jobs-lite" businesses

New thinking about career progression

It becomes apparent that simply considering your next job is not going to be enough. We need to strategize your future so that one job aligns you for your next position and the one after that.

Strategic thinking here mandates a progression of three positions. Usually, jobseekers think from their current place and moving upward. However, in this kind of NewThink, a different direction will be far more helpful and fruitful.

In the visual below: the top orange circles are opportunities that are six to eight years in the future. The middle circles are those positions three to four years in the future. And the lowest row represents current opportunities.

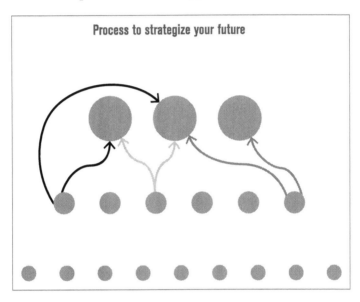

Process to strategize your future

These hierarchies, in some instances, may be quite obvious. For example, a person may work as operations support staff (bottom row). This could lead to an assistant manager (middle row) and then to a full manager (top row). In the same way, a manager position may lead to a director appointment.

From any position, a person may move to a different company that is larger or into a different industry. Examples:

- A sales manager moves from a small regional company to a medium company with a national presence.

- A business analyst may move from a departmental position in one company to an analyst position for an entire business unit.

Hence, the title from a position in the lowest row may not change when moving to a position in the middle. However, the astute jobseeker, keeping a careful eye on the industry and on competing companies, may move to a new company with greater opportunity—and continue with the same title. In the new position, there will be greater responsibilities (and a better income!).

The arrows in the visual indicate that one opportunity prepares or aligns with the position above it. So the arrows show potential career growth. Establishing these arrows becomes important when moving down to the lower tier.

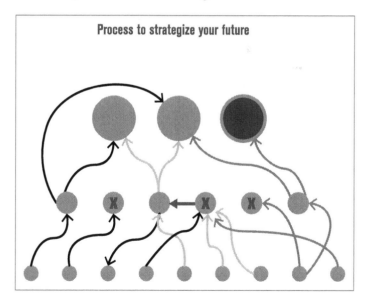

Process to strategize your future

In this image we see the importance of tracking career growth for at least three positions. We can easily see the potential opportunities and risks:

- The arrows from the lowest tier show potential movement to future possibilities.

- The circles marked X indicate a dead end. These second-tier positions do not lead anywhere and should be avoided. Those positions may once have led to a better job, but the situation has changed.

- Realizing that a position has no upward or forward mobility mandates a lateral move to ensure a better position for the next career move. The black arrow, pointing to the left indicates a potential lateral move to align for the next career move.

- The circle in the upper right corner has gone dark. That means that a potential opportunity has disappeared. So the next career move would likely be a lateral move or a focus on another opportunity alignment.

From this discussion, it becomes clear that tracking career possibilities at least two positions forward is critical. At the writing of this book, this time frame is approximately three to four years between positions. Choosing not to track industry movement is tantamount to flying a plane during tornado season without checking the weather.

These images have nice neat circles, straight lines, and a clear spacing. It is probably far from the reality that most people will experience. Disruptive innovations, changes in the global markets, weather, and general business dysfunction will each play a part as many try to keep up with the rate of change—some, many, or all of these will require career trackers to be aware, agile, and especially resilient.

As we move into the future, the three-to-four-year time frame could change. It is possible that as technology advances, tech jobs might last no longer than six to nine months. IT professionals may find that they work for six months and train in new technologies for three months. This cycle might be a repeated reality.

Regardless of changes in the future, this career model will serve as your plan to navigate the challenges you will likely face.. Checking this plan every quarter is highly recommended. Later in the book, we will discuss changes within industries and within companies that signal new directions are on the horizon.

► Consequently, it bears repeating that career planning is the responsibility of the jobseeker and not the employer.

Although the images above show perfect circles and colorful lines, the reality of a career path will likely be messy. The person who says, "I've been incredibly fortunate that good jobs have always come my way, and together, they have created a perfect career for me!" is indeed the exception.

A career path is most likely to be challenging, messy, unpredictable, and in constant need of care and attention.

If you are in your early or mid-career, it is fairly easy to see the application of this model to your future. Although this model may look "corporate," it really isn't. The hierarchy is about your goals and ensuring there are options for your future. The model is about the availability of jobs and aligning your current situation to ensure you don't hit a dead end.

Perhaps you are a senior executive who has already achieved "C-Suite" status. If that is the case, the model still works. Your top circles may include owning your own consulting business or being a senior contributor to a top consulting firm. It could also include a leadership role in the nonprofit sector.

To maintain a consistent income, it is important to remember the basic process:

1. Identify ideal job possibilities.

2. Ensure there is a market for them.

3. Strategize two career moves into the future.

The previous section described the process to think two career moves into the future. The next two sections describe a process to clearly understand your ideal job possibilities across different industries and ensure there is a market. These two steps will set you up to prioritize a current jobsearch, even if you are currently employed.

New thinking: Characteristics of an Ideal Job

You might be tempted to skip this section. Many people believe that they know what a "good" job is. Yet when they are asked, they begin countless stories about positions that were no good, and they may describe times in their work history where they truly enjoyed certain aspects of a particular job. However, finding a person with a clear definition of what constitutes a good job is the exception—even among long-term jobseekers.

The time it takes to clearly identify what makes a job "good" is time well spent. Without it, it is impossible to truly evaluate an opportunity or a job offer. Jobseekers who understand these key components can reduce their search and their effort by applying only for those jobs that fit. Again, these are particular to every jobseeker—rather than the job. Retrofitting a job to a jobseeker is a lot harder than the other way around. It almost never works.

Further, one of the biggest blunders that jobseekers make is talking to their network *before* they know what they are looking for. The consequence is that their greatest advocates have been misdirected and don't know how to help them.

How to identify your ideal position

Earlier in this section a good job was described as one that is satisfying, sustainable, and financially manageable. This section brings a process to find these kinds of positions.

Most people want a job that is meaningful and a place that values specific traits from their core personality. Contrarily, many people have developed skills that they don't really enjoy. Although they are capable of performing certain functions, if such activities make up a large percentage of the job, it isn't a good fit!

Finally, "work environment" is a critical and often over-looked component of an ideal job. This becomes an essential if not a central part of enjoyment. Doing what you love in a toxic environment can result in losing your enjoyment for that particular activity. Doing something that isn't ideal, but with people who genuinely care about quality and excellence as well as each other—that can be far preferable.

The key elements of a job that fits include your:

- Values

- Attributes

- Skills

- Environment

Clear definition of these key elements provides a set of guides for evaluating potential career tracks and job opportunities. These are personal components that indicate job fit for the individual. No two people will have the exact same traits. They will be discussed in detail later in this section. Conveniently, they spell VASE.

Although personal traits may define a description of job fit for the individual, they are of little value if there is no place for them in the job market. By themselves, they are not enough to give career direction. The two missing components include:

1. Specific industries where personal traits are needed and

2. The job market itself.

The following graphic shows a formula that combines the personal traits of an individual integrated into a specific industry to form a composite that can be compared to the current job market.

Your personal traits may change or shift, and skill sets will change as you develop new skills and unused skills fade. However, every time an industry dies or morphs into something new and every time the job market changes, your career track will need to be adjusted to ensure a consistent income stream. As the authors have consistently emphasized, industries and job markets are in a continuous cycle of change.

Formula for Credible Career Opportunities

Values
+
Attributes
+
Skills
+
Environment

+ Your Industry ÷ Job Market

Example: At the writing of this book:

1. Many marketing professionals are struggling to find opportunity. One reason is that their industry has changed due to social media. High-level jobs

disappeared as companies tried to decipher and embrace the buying behaviors of new consumers. The marketing industry changed, and the job market dried up.

2. A high school grad went to college and studied to be a newspaper reporter. He graduated in four years only to find that social media completely changed the process by which stories were selected, created, and reported. Tablet technology captured the print industry, and newspapers were closing down their print editions. Traditional reporters were no longer needed.

3. A movie producer worked for 25 years directing videos for large corporations to use as promotional and informational marketing as well as corporate communications. The Great Recession reduced budgets, the video quality of smartphones made producers of everyone, and the public preference shifted to "reality TV and video." Together, these three changes all but closed down his industry.

► Consequently, it bears repeating that career planning and job fit are the responsibility of the jobseeker and not the employer.

It is critically important to complete the process to clearly understand the attributes of a job that fits. If you are unemployed, the temptation to take any job is heavy, and that may be a temporary solution. However, in the long run, it is a poor choice and a risky compromise.

Finding jobs that fit

This process has been created to help you identify your values, attributes, skills, and optimum work environment. The goal is to create a clear definition of the characteristics of jobs in which you will enjoy your work, bring value, and earn a reliable income.

As you go through this process, you will identify many characteristics that you prefer in a perfect employment situation. We all know that employers do not seek to put together jobs that meet our criteria. Besides, all jobs have aspects that a person would rather do without. However, knowing your preferences and prioritizing them will serve you in several ways:

- It will be possible to potentially negotiate your current situation.

- Knowing what is ideal helps jobseekers select jobs that are a good fit before they apply.

- Knowing there is no perfect job, this process allows a person to evaluate a job offer.

Generally speaking, if a person has approximately 65 to 75 percent of their optimum preferences, the job is likely to be a good fit.

VALUES: Jobs with meaning!

Finding meaningful work has been a challenge for a vast majority of jobseekers. Yet there are numerous ways that people find meaning in their work. Here are five; all are credible and valid.

Values: What brings meaning?

 It's the "end receivers" of the work effort

 Hands-on each day

 A part of something bigger

 Within the workplace

 Means to an end

1. The "end receiver" is valued

    . . . and therefore brings meaning to the daily work.

    Example: A database manager loves animals, especially dogs (she owns six). Not wanting to return to the corporate environment, she landed a job working for the International Humane Society in their IT department. She doesn't work with or interact with animals, but her job has meaning because she knows that many animals are better off because of her work.

2. Day-to-day work with the receiver.

   This includes any position that works directly with receivers. Examples include teachers, medical staff, including nurses, doctors, homecare aides, and x-ray technicians. Also included are sales staff and customer service representatives.

3. Being a part of something bigger.

   This can be expressed in many different ways and at different levels within an organization. For example, a person may find value in the insurance industry because having good insurance at a critical time in his or her life, or the life of someone they know, prevented some kind of catastrophic loss.

   Similarly, a person might work with a team of legal advisers for nonprofits. The value comes from the need of many nonprofits to get good legal advice and secure their ability to serve their various constituencies. Other people may have a "cause" that is important to them, such as the environment or underserved populations, such as the homeless or animal species that are at risk.

4. Simply making the workplace better for those who work there.

   A vast number of workers enjoy the relationship aspect of their work. They may, in some way, be the hub—the person everyone goes to when they need something. In that moment, this person seizes the opportunity to assist, encourage, fix—and, of course, follow up to ensure they have been helpful. The context is less important. This kind of value also includes experts in their field, who find value by giving away their expertise.

There are two categories of "making the workplace better." One includes the physical workplace, and the other includes the virtual workplace where an expertise is needed. Examples of these positions include receptionist, help-desk/customer service, administrative assistant, author, commentator . . . any expert at any level.

5. For many people, their job is a means to an end. It serves as a vehicle to provide for their families and to enjoy a lifestyle of their choosing. This doesn't mean that they don't care about their job. They may be some of the most engaged, driven people in the office or workplace. They protect their paycheck and the peace of mind they have that they can manage their life.

All these methods of finding value at work are credible and legitimate. Everyone has limits or boundaries where they will not work. For example, just the fact that the job is a means to an end doesn't mean a person would be happy working in the tobacco industry. One client indicated that the merchant services industry was "dirty" and he wanted out of it. (Merchant services provide credit card processing for businesses.)

So the question remains, how do you identify your values?

 Identifying your values

At first, you might think that you already know what you value. However, it is likely that there are many values that you haven't thought about, and these values may very well open up ideas that might not otherwise have occurred to you.

There are several ways to go about identifying your values. The process offered here may help.

1. Begin a list and ask these questions:

    - What part of your work life do you enjoy the most?
    - What accomplishments are you proud of?
    - What makes for a good day at work?
    - What contributes to feeling good about your work?

Translate your answers: If you indicated you are proud of a mended relationship, then **relationships** are part of your values. If you are proud of being the top sales leader in your area, then you value **accomplishment, recognition,** *and* what you see as your actions that brought about the recognition. That could mean your **negotiation** skills, your **collaborative** manner, and your ability to build **trust** and **influence** decision makers.

Perhaps a good day at work is focused on your "deliverables" or what you accomplished. That could be a computer application, a report, or the details for a work event. If that is the case, you value what you accomplished *and* the tools you used to accomplish them. For example, if someone felt good about finishing up a report, they value **completing projects.** They may also value **details** that bring **credibility** to the report. If they collected information from others, then they may also value **collaboration** as well as the **relationships** with people across business units or within their industry.

2. This partial list of values may help get you started.

• Achievement	• Community	• Independence
• Autonomy	• Collaboration	• Leadership
• Advancement	• Cooperation	• Loyalty
• Challenge	• Decisiveness	• Organization
• Change, variety	• Growth	• Public service
• Relationships	• Honesty, integrity	• Reputation

3. Another way to put together your list is to simply conduct an Internet search on "values."

ATTRIBUTES: Jobs that fit naturally!

Have you ever met someone and the two of you just seemed to "hit it off"? Somehow there was good chemistry. Communication was easy, the atmosphere was relaxed, and laughter was spontaneous.

Jobs that fit are similar in that the work environment needs your natural predispositions or attributes. Attributes are those characteristics that are with you no matter where you are.

Examples include a sense of humor and an ability to generate ideas or synthesize large quantities of information. Jobs that utilize your natural attributes quickly become a natural fit.

 Identifying your attributes

Attributes can be a bit tricky. Since they are such an innate part of who we are, we often don't think about them. They developed as we grew up and matured. Sometimes they are so much a part of us that we may not identify them, and we may not realize that these characteristics are valuable in the work environment.

There are several ways to go about identifying your attributes. The process offered here may help. This process is similar to identifying your values.

1. Begin a list and ask these questions:

    • How would your family and close friends describe you?

    • How about your colleagues?

    • What have your managers or supervisors listed as your top contributions?

    • What about when you are with people you don't know, but interact with, such as the grocery store checkout person, the person who answers the phone when you call technical support?

    Consider having a conversation with some people, and ask them how they would describe you. What are your best attributes?

2. This partial list may get you started.

• Adaptable	• Good listener	• Logical, practical
• Analytical	• Diplomatic	• Mediator
• Cheerful, pleasant	• Creative, imaginative	• Persuasive
• Dependable	• Focused	• Open minded
• Enthusiastic	• Independent	• Organized
• Flexible	• Leader	• Patient

3. Another way to put together your list is to simply conduct an Internet search on "personal attributes." You will find very long lists, and some may seem quite comprehensive. This may be one of those times where too much information isn't helpful. Suggestion: look for lists that are condensed: "The top 10 personal attributes" and the like.

SKILLS: What you will do each day

Marcia: I believe that today, most people have several sets of skills rather that one set of skills. Skills can be divided in a variety of ways. We often hear about "soft skills" such as relationship building and negotiation in contrast to hard skills such as computer programming, software management, and specific industry expertise.

Here's the concern: Most people can do many things well. They may be fast and efficient, but that doesn't mean that they enjoy those tasks. As I've mentioned earlier, when a large percentage of the skills needed to do the job fall in the "I-don't-really-care-that-much" category, then the job loses its enjoyment, and the employee becomes disengaged.

I believe that the concerns about these well-developed skills that aren't important stems from early in our lives. Do you remember when you were young and people would ask, "What do you want to be when you grow up?" For me it was an awkward question. I don't remember wanting to "be" something; I wanted to "do" stuff.

Today, I still believe that it was the wrong question. When I began studying how careers developed, I found that most people don't think about the activities they enjoy when they decide to apply for a position. Instead, their thoughts are considering the potential raise, the promotion, and so forth. Although such considerations are important, other factors should be added to the equation.

Our sets of skills should include a combination:

1. What we enjoy,

2. What we do well, and

3. What is in high demand by current employers.

I'm going to use myself as an example. Most of my college training was in music. I studied, practiced, and earned degrees in orchestral conducting, classical composition, and adult music education. It may sound glamorous, but the truth is that for the last fifteen years, there hasn't been much demand for *any* of those things. Nonetheless, I've been able to extract sets of skills and earn a consistent living.

Here are a few examples of how my skills were adapted to take advantage of my past experience and what I enjoyed and integrate them into the market.

- Part of music conducting is learning the music and then identifying problems and making corrections during rehearsal. Those skills are needed for software quality assurance work. I learned about the personal lines auto insurance business and then found "bugs" in the software that determined the customer premiums.
- Orchestra rehearsals and performance translated to corporate training (i.e., getting adults to do something better and collaborate to raise excellence). I became a corporate trainer in the world of mutual funds. The "performance" for me was training new call-center reps to be excited and engaged as they helped brokers and clients with their financial portfolios.
- Every concert is, by classic definition, a project: It has a specified start date, an end date (the concert), scope (the choice of music), and resources (how many musicians can be hired at what rate and for how many rehearsals). I translated this into the corporate world and became a project manager for a Fortune 50 company. I managed the effort to develop training for a new project management methodology.

Obviously skills are of paramount importance to qualify you for a job. However, we need to look carefully at what we like and what we do well and match the results with the current jobs market, to ensure a consistent income.

NOTE: We now differentiate between the "commerce" and e-commerce market, and the jobs market. We have also referred to other markets such as the housing market. At this point, the difference is an important one.

Obviously, as companies (of any size) adapt to meet changes in their customers' needs, the skills needed to meet those needs will change with the adaptation. To maintain a personal income, we need to watch trends, be aware of changes, and capitalize on and adapt our sets of skills to remain relevant. Otherwise, we will soon be looking for a job.

So with these thoughts in mind, we can return to our quest to define our sets of skills. And the question is "What do you like to do?"

 Identifying your skills

Your list should not be limited to your work life. Think broadly, and include everything you can think of, even in your childhood. Our natural inclinations draw us in, and we naturally develop skills that are easy to overlook.

1. Begin a comprehensive list by asking these questions. (NOTE: Some of these have been asked before, but for different reasons.)

   • What part of your work life do you enjoy the most?

   • What was accomplished?

   • What were you doing that was enjoyable?

   • When you were young, what did you like to do best?

   • What activities did you like to do when you were in school? College? Leisure time? With friends?

As you begin to compile your comprehensive list, begin to sort them into categories. Some entries will fit into several of the categories.

2. Here are some activities, sorted into possible categories:

Soft skills	Hard skills	Independent skills	Collaboration skills
• Active listening	• Customer service	• Documentation	• Negotiation
• Critical thinking	• Mathematics	• Complex problem solving	• Marketing
• Customer service	• Presentations	• Decision-making	• Operations management
• Management skills	• Research	• Writing	• Process design
• Negotiation	• Systems analysis	• Editing	• Meeting management
• Cooperation	• Programming	• Fact-checking	• Product development
• Observation	• Technology management	• Research	• Planning
• Focus	• Communication	• Following procedures	
• Communication	• Organization	• Planning	

3. Search the Internet to find lists of skills. You can search for soft skills, hard skills, technical skills, customer service skills, etc. You might even look up some job postings for positions that you have had in the past to see how the skills for that position are specified.

NOTE: Oftentimes, lists for soft skills will include natural attributes. For our purposes, look for activities that you would perform while on the job.

ENVIRONMENT: How you are most effective!

In the past, many people didn't think much about their work environment. Since the Great Recession of 2008, that has changed. The severe layoffs in the Great Recession caused many work environments to become toxic. As many will attest, more and more people were laid off, and the quantity of work remained unchanged. This caused workloads to double and triple on those people who were retained. CEOs were pressed to increase profit margins, which caused a domino effect of stress to inundate and overwhelm the entire company.

A deep price was paid to keep companies from collapse. As this trend continued, employees became exhausted and disengaged. As a result, jobseekers have become keenly aware of the quality of their work environment. At the writing of this book, the key phrase in the corporate hiring world is "employee engagement." So we are seeing a turnaround, and employers are focusing on providing a better work environment to increase the quality of completed work.

When considering "environment," we tend to think of the emotional attitude or culture. There is more to it than that. Few people consider whether they work best with a small team or a core group that reaches out to form relationships across the business. Perhaps they like to work independently most of the time but as part of a larger team. Some people have a need to know the impact of their work on the broader business goals in order to successfully do their job; others, not so much.

Studies show that some people prefer to have ambient noise while they work. It could be a radio, TV, or simply the sounds of other employees. Another optimum work indicator is the office space itself. Some people work better in large spaces; others prefer a confined area that they control. Some prefer to stand, while others prefer cushy chairs. Studies also indicate that some people prefer to have a hot drink, others a cold drink, and others like both within reach.

This brings up additional questions, and the answers significantly contribute to your optimum work environment. The ones that I find most important are in questions one and two.

 Identifying your optimum environment

Now we are going to ask questions to help determine your optimum work environment.

1. On average, how many people are you with when you do your best work?
   a. Best when you are by yourself?
   b. Four or less?
   c. About six to ten?
   d. More than ten?

2. Do you prefer a mixture of independent, small team, and larger group? What is the mix?
   a. Work by yourself and with a small core group (how many) that you interact with daily?
   b. Work by yourself and with a small core group that you interact with occasionally (how often)?
   c. Work by yourself and with a large group on occasion (how many, how often)?
   d. Work with a core group daily and a larger group on occasion (how many, how often)?

3. How do I connect best with others in the workplace?
   a. Face to face
   b. Phone
   c. E-mail
   d. Virtual meetings
   e. Real-time

4. Now determine the percentages between your "alone" time and that which is spent in meetings, on the phone, in training, etc. Here are a few examples:
   a. 25% gathering requirements from leadership, 75% research (independently gathering data) and analysis.
   b. 60% in meetings, 25% with a core team, 15% alone for strategic thinking.
   c. 85% managing the call center and supporting the CSRs, 15% reporting and escalating issues.
   d. 15% identifying training needs with management, 40% developing and testing training, 35% delivering training, 10% reporting.

5. What about your immediate work space? Which do you prefer?
   a. Small area I can control.
   b. Larger area with ambient sound.
   c. Quiet!
   d. Bright light.
   e. Warm light.
   f. ?

6. What volume of work do you prefer?
   a. Moderate to heavy workload.
   b. I work best when there is a fire to put out.
   c. Breakneck speed?
   d. Slow and careful to ensure accuracy.
   e. A variety: times of intensity and other times with a moderate work flow.

7. How much autonomy do you prefer?
   a. I prefer to know exactly how something should be done. Micromanaging helps me ensure I am doing my job well.
   b. Once I understand the goal, leave me alone, and I'll exceed your expectations. If I have a question, I'll ask.
   c. I prefer to check in on a regular basis to ensure the project is on the right track.

8. What kind of organization do you prefer?
   a. Non-profit?
   b. Academic setting?
   c. Non-governmental Organization (NGO)?
   d. Corporate?
   e. Small or medium sized business?
   f. Retail and Service sector?
   g. Manufacturing?
   h. Start-up company?

As you complete your lists, you may find repetition of some words and phrases in each of the four categories. If the same words or phrases appear in three of the four categories, then it likely ranks high on your list of "must haves" for a job to be a good fit.

But it isn't exciting

This is a good place in our process to remind ourselves that excitement, interest, and enjoyment about a job come from different motivators. Again, our values are what bring meaning to our work. Here is a quick review from the values section:

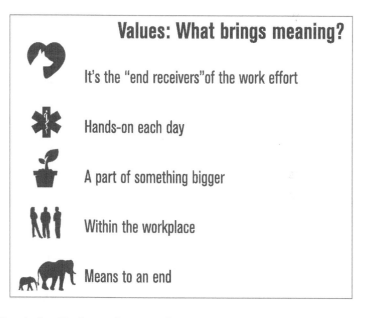

Values: What brings meaning?

It's the "end receivers" of the work effort

Hands-on each day

A part of something bigger

Within the workplace

Means to an end

Reminder: Doing what you love in a toxic environment can quickly result in losing your enjoyment for that particular activity. Doing something that isn't ideal but doing it with people who are engaged and care about quality and excellence as well as each other—that can be far preferable.

Ensuring your place in the jobs market

At this point you should have a clear definition of your values, attributes, skills, and optimal environment that together describe a job opportunity that is a good fit for you. Most people, at this stage, realize that their skills can be used in numerous ways and in a wide variety of positions.

The next step is to ensure a market is waiting to hire you and that it will meet your financial needs. These two factors, the market and your financial needs, will help you narrow down your viable options and identify the audience of your jobsearch toolset.

When teaching jobseekers to find opportunities online, I generally ask them to prioritize each of their VASE results (values, attributes, skills, and environment); then we add a list of industries where they have experience. Then we search for positions by testing word sets, using these lists. We almost always use an industry and an attribute and then another word. We search globally until we find word sets that bring in jobs that are a good fit. Then we add a geographic location to the mix.

The following are some examples of words sets that we might use:

Values	Attributes	Skills	Environment	Industry
Environment	Creative	Writing	Team	Insurance
Animals	Positive	Outside sales	Independent	Manufacturing
Children	Humor	Research	Liaison	Finance
Education	Professional	Teaching	Collaboration	Biotech

The rules are:

- If there are too few results, use fewer words.
- If there are too many results, add words.
- If the results do not fit, use different words.

We mix and match the words to find jobs that fit. It can take a while, but the result is that everyone finds that there are more jobs that they can do and that interest them than they ever imagined. A more detailed explanation of the jobsearch process follows shortly.

At the writing of this book, one way of identifying open employment opportunities is through job boards. As technology has matured, specifically the applicant tracking systems (ATS), more and more emphasis has been placed on applying for positions through online means. Most people approach these with a job title in mind. If they are a business analyst or a project manager, then they use those terms to identify potential positions.

This approach may work with some positions, but the search results can be extensive, and the jobseeker will spend a lot of time looking through an ocean of positions. An additional concern is that job titles are not standardized. Although most positions with a title of "business analyst" will likely be just that, other positions with differing titles will be missed which might be a better fit.

Example:

I searched indeed.com with the terms: Business Analyst . . . as you might have guessed, almost every position had those words in the job title. Here are some examples of the results:

- Client Services Business Analyst
- Business Analyst
- IS Business Analyst
- Junior Level Business Analyst
- Entry Level Business Analyst

My second search used the terms: analysis technical creative. The results were much different and included:

- Product Manager (entry level)
- Solutions Consultant
- Report Developer
- Technical Software Consultant
- Technical Writer, Senior
- Implementation Specialist

So we see that if we only use job titles for our jobsearch, then we are going to limit our results, and we won't have a consistent idea of the jobs market that enables us to compare our searches and prioritize by job availability. In other words, we want to know where the jobs are that match our top interests. If we have a keen interest in something, but there are only a few jobs, then we want to know that up front and prioritize our jobsearch accordingly.

The process is quite simple. By conducting a jobsearch through an aggregator search engine (described below), we can identify how many jobs there are in certain sectors and locations. So the process is this:

1. Identify keywords that bring results of jobs that are a good fit.

2. Check to see how many jobs are available "globally" and then locally.

Granted, this process may not include positions that are managed through the so-called "hidden jobs market"—i.e., retained search firms—and it will not include positions that are not advertised. However, our goal here is simply to ensure that there is a market for our intended jobsearch.

Finding job opportunities

Finding viable positions takes a bit of experimentation to identify the right words to find the right jobs. But the results make it worth the effort. If you have completed the activities in this section, then you probably have the words you need to find the right positions and identify the jobs market for the kind of job you want.

1. At the writing of this book, there are several types of job boards:
   a. Aggregators (they search the web daily for job postings)

    b. Boutique job boards (specific to an industry or job role, e.g., technology, nonprofits, manufacturing)

    c. Company websites

    d. Business social sites such as LinkedIn and Glassdoor.com

NOTE: At this point we are identifying the text strings that will bring in jobs that are a good fit for you. We are not yet ready to attract recruiters and other hiring professionals.

2. Search globally. It doesn't matter where the job is located, since we are simply identifying the word sets that will bring in jobs that are a good fit.

3. Begin with three or four words. Generally, this includes an industry, an attribute, a skill, and a "wild card." Here are some examples:

    a. Finance analytical research diplomatic

    b. Insurance enthusiastic negotiation pets

    c. Nonprofit creative write persuasive

    d. Education practical mediation program

    e. Technology flexible programmer team-leader

4. Rules:

    a. If you don't get enough results, then remove one word.

    b. If you get too many results, add another word.

    c. If you get results that are not a good match, change your word set.

GOAL: The goal is to:

1. Find jobs that are a good fit and
2. Ensure there is a market for those jobs.

As mentioned earlier, this takes some experimentation. However, many word sets can be quickly eliminated because the initial results are not a good match.

Once you find word sets that bring up jobs that meet your criteria, check the number of positions that are available. Track the number of positions both nationally and locally. Ideally, you should have three or four sets of words that bring positions that are a good fit.

These sets of words will likely identify positions in different career tracks but for which you still qualify. In my search, there were three separate career tracks: project management, corporate training, and director of operations. When it was time to develop résumés, three basic templates were created. Each one emphasized the elements in my background that were important to that particular track. This will be discussed later in the book.

Check the examples below for the marketability of positions brought up through the search: analysis technical creative. The one on the top is a national search, and there are 16,784 available positions in the United States. In the state of Connecticut, there are 180 positions, and in Hartford, there are 119 positions. Connecticut is a very small state, located between Boston and New York City. It's possible to drive most places in the state in about two hours.

A different set of words may also bring up positions that are in a different career track. If there are more positions available in other searches, then the market is better and you might want to prioritize your search accordingly.

Misleading hiring cycles

Before we leave this section on how to find job opportunities through job boards, there is another factor that often misleads jobseekers—the hiring cycles.

At the writing of this book, about 65 percent of companies in the U.S. use the calendar year as their fiscal year. So their reporting year begins on January 1 and ends on December 31.

That means that by fourth quarter, most companies have determined their budgets and projects for the coming year. That means they know what resources will be needed to accomplish those projects. This starts a wave of job postings in an attempt to get as much in place before the year-end holidays as possible. In other words, there is a hiring-spree! (This counters the idea of many jobseekers that they are okay to take a break in their jobsearch from the end of November through mid-January.)

After the postings are published, candidates are selected for the interview process. During this time, there are very few new job postings on the online job boards. This lull in activity can be unnerving to jobseekers.

Once the first set of candidates has been selected, they resign their current positions—which leaves a new set of positions that need to be filled. So the cycle begins again: jobs are posted followed by a lull in activity as candidates are selected and interviewed. The cycle repeats again and again until the need is exhausted. I call this the ebb and flow of the hiring cycle.

When jobseekers search online for potential job announcements, they must know where they are in the hiring cycle. In the example below, arrows B and D indicate where numerous job openings are posted to online job boards. Arrows A and C show the lull in activity while candidates are screened and interviewed.

What happens if the jobseeker looks for jobs only during the A and C time frames? There will be very few jobs available, and the jobseeker may think that the market for those positions isn't as good as the market for other positions—and that may be a false assessment.

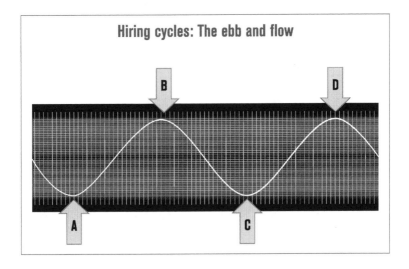

Hiring cycles: The ebb and flow

Therefore, it's critical to know the hiring cycles for positions that interest you and ensure that you are looking for opportunities during the "high-tide" in the cycle.

The hiring cycle can differ in length depending on the industry. The cycle in the insurance industry in 2008 was approximately three months. So jobs were posted for approximately one month to six weeks, and then came a lull of about the same length. Jobseekers panicked when the number of positions dried up—fearful that there were no more jobs. At the writing of this book, the cycle is approximately two weeks for some industries such as IT support, Call-center customer service, and so forth.

It should be obvious that the number of available positions and the length of the hiring cycle are also determined by the type of position. There are fewer C-Suite positions than there are, say, for business analysts. So the hiring cycle for business analysts will likely be shorter than that of senior executives.

An earlier statement indicated that 65 percent of companies use the calendar year as their fiscal year. The remaining 35 percent of companies maintain the traditional fiscal year that begins on July 1 and continues to June 30. The calendar shifts, but the principle remains the same in terms of their hiring cycles.

Career management review

There are three critical elements that jobseekers must have before they initiate a jobsearch—an ability to:

1. Identify ideal job possibilities,

2. Ensure there is a market for them, and

3. Strategize two career moves into the future.

Here is the graphic on strategizing two moves into the future:

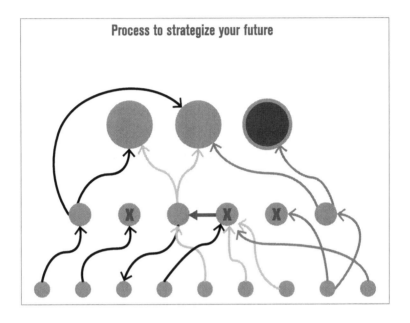

Process to strategize your future

The main point is to find opportunities in the bottom row that will align you for at least two moves forward.

PART THREE

JOBSEARCH AND CAREER MANAGEMENT PRINCIPLES

As you begin this section, it is assumed that you:

- Can list the characteristics of a job that is a good fit.
- Know how to recognize and articulate those characteristics.
- Can identify employment opportunities that you qualify for in the hopes of being considered in the hiring process.

New sets of skills for jobsearch and career management

During the 2008 Great Recession, the hiring process underwent tremendous upheaval. With so many jobseekers clamoring for jobs, technology took on a major role in the selection process. Social media brought new connectivity to relationships, and the Internet enabled businesses to have a global outreach. New skills were identified by businesses, as were a new set of hiring practices and a process to evaluate changing company needs.

The new technology of applicant tracking systems (ATS) enabled businesses to publish employment opportunities around the world, and they could now receive and process enormous numbers of applications. The competition to be considered for a position rose exponentially. The ability of a jobseeker to differentiate him- or herself became a number one priority, and it will remain so for the foreseeable future. Keeping up with the new technologies associated with the ever-changing hiring practices has become a skill set in itself.

The availability of social connectivity on various platforms (business as well as personal) adds another dimension to career management, and it will continue to evolve and mature and play a role in the elimination of candidates for potential positions. That makes "social" a primary factor for the jobseeker and adds another skill set that has to be developed and managed.

For jobseekers and employees who are carefully managing their careers, LinkedIn is the primary social media platform for business as this book is written. An Internet search on the life expectancy of social media platforms brought up a scientific study indicating that platforms would likely last approximately ten years. *http://davidamerland.com/seo-blog/941-the-life-expectancy-of-a-social-network.html.*

This does not mean that social media are going away or that LinkedIn, Twitter, and Facebook will fail or close. It does mean that these platforms will likely give way to a new generation of connectivity, and it is up to each individual (whether employed or looking for work) to be on top of the trend. Here is a list of considerations:

- Understand how social media are being used by the hiring communities.
- Remain current in these new, technology-driven modes of connectivity.
- Manage your presence to your advantage.
- Update a carefully crafted strategy to secure and maintain your online professional presence.
- Ensure your "presence" demonstrates those skill sets that are current and relevant to business communities.
- Your social "presence" should be in sync with your résumé and support a cohesive and integrated script

Because social media are in the public domain, what you post there can and most likely will be examined by the recruiters and HR professionals that have an interest in you.

A survey in 2014 by Jobvite indicated that 94 percent of recruiters use LinkedIn while only 36 percent of jobseekers use it. We believe that the use of social media will only increase as our online "presence" becomes a professional asset. *http://money.usnews.com/money/careers/articles/2015/02/19/ what-recruiters-think-when-they-see-your-linkedin-profile*

Anything you have posted online which might show you in an unfavorable light to a potential employer has to be removed from your social media profiles.

It becomes apparent that as social media platforms evolve, hiring professionals will utilize them to increase their ability to find the right people. Details on using these platforms are intentionally left out of this book because best practices are changing so quickly. We believe that this information can be found through online venues and is a part of every person's career management life cycle.

General advice regarding social media

Although specific best practices are changing, some specific advice will not likely become outdated.

1. Keep photos up to date. These should be headshots (shoulders up) and in professional dress.

2. Connectivity is critical, and engagement with people on social platforms with regard to business expertise will support your candidacy.

3. Sharing content is a form of engagement and is highly recommended.

4. Following companies and thought leaders in your industry and areas of expertise will be an asset and represent you well with hiring professionals.

5. Regularly research current best practices with regard to overused words. Words like "passionate" and "results driven" become overused. A quick Internet search will give you the current list. Update your profiles on a regular basis.

Career management skills and tools

The hiring process is continually changing, and failure to follow current trends will result in a delay or gap in employment. It is evident to every jobseeker that hiring communities expect specific skills and specific tools. Although these skills and tools are specific to the writing of this book, the basic function of the skills will not change.

The product that jobseekers use to demonstrate their credibility for employment opportunities will change with business needs, hiring processes and the development of technology. For example, many IT and marketing companies give potential candidates a tech problem or a case study and ask them to build code or create a marketing strategy. This gives them the opportunity to demonstrate their abilities.

Here are lists for consideration. These skills, mandated by the hiring community to meet their needs, will likely remain for decades to come. The jobseeker will need to adapt the method of responding to these needs to whatever platforms are in current use.

Career Management Skills and Tools	
EXPECTED SKILLS BY HR	**CAREER MANAGEMENT TOOLS**
Ability to find employment opportunities utilizing online jobsearch platforms.	Online jobsearch account management, professional e-mail management. A searchable personal database (e.g., MSExcel) to track history and progress of both jobsearch, recruiter connectivity, networking, job applications, and their status.

Career Management Skills and Tools	
EXPECTED SKILLS BY HR	**CAREER MANAGEMENT TOOLS**
Ability to connect appropriately with hiring professionals.	Consistent professional demeanor, both in written and spoken language. E-mail and other online communication tools (e.g., Google Hangouts, SKYPE, Facetime, videotaped interview/screening sessions).
Ability to present polished, relevant, accurate documentation of current credibility regarding employment.	Polished, customizable, accurate cover letter and résumé. Possible trends: A video/audio resume.
Appropriate online presence that supports the documentation of employment and skills and professional expertise.	LinkedIn or other/newer social business media accounts: up to date and with relevant, current activity. Recommendations from past employers, staff, colleagues, and other professionals. An online presence as demonstrated by activity in professional groups, online chat rooms, blogs, presentations, and volunteer work. A network of professionals, both online and in-person relationships.
Validation of factual information found on the employment application.	Transcripts, certification documentation, references, recommendations, tax documentation of previous income.
An ability to credibly manage any documentation concerns of the hiring community. I.e., employment gaps, health concerns, credit or legal concerns, driving record, and liability insurance.	These are all dependent on individual circumstances. A professional career coach may be an excellent investment for learning how to manage each concern to the satisfaction of hiring professionals.
An ability to pass background checks that are appropriate to the industry and/or positions being considered.	

134

Case studies

The names in these studies have been changed.

Botched video interview

Sarah was delighted to receive an e-mail requesting an interview. The e-mail indicated that the interview would be online and she would need to activate the camera and microphone on her computer. A link was provided, and she assumed that she would be asked to schedule her interview.

She clicked on the link and to her dismay, she was directed not to touch her computer while the "meeting" was set up. The camera light on her computer indicated that it had been activated, and a voice indicated the interview was about to begin. There she sat in her sweats rather than professional dress. She had just washed her hair, which was still wrapped in a towel. Her mind was going at light speed as she realized that she had applied to two jobs at this company and did not know which job she was being interviewed for.

The first question was typical as the voice asked her to talk about herself and informed her that she would have 60 seconds to respond. The questions became more and more involved as she was asked how her skill sets directly related to the particular position—which was not mentioned!

After thirty minutes, the interview was over. Two minutes later she received an e-mail indicating she would not be moving forward in the hiring process.

Sarah was stunned, unnerved, and frustrated. She reread the e-mail and realized that there was nothing there that would have prepared her for the online interview. Nothing from the company website or in their communications set her expectations. The longer she thought about it, the angrier she became.

She called the company and tried to connect with the hiring professionals. In the end, she was told that their hiring process was carefully designed, and nothing could be done about it. Sarah realized that her demeanor in her communications about the experience carried overtones of her frustration and resentment.

This scenario describes a nightmare by any stretch of the imagination. Once a company reaches out for an interview, jobseekers should consider online watchdog groups that may give them needed information to prevent such catastrophes. Glassdoor.com offers information about company culture, salaries, and the interview experience as offered by jobseekers. In addition, a jobseeker can search for current and former employees through resources such as LinkedIn. Many people will gladly give someone fifteen minutes of their time to help out. These kinds of conversations can be easily scheduled *if* jobseekers reach out at the time they apply to positions and can then reconnect if an interview is forthcoming.

Video résumés have not been adopted by the hiring community at large. That doesn't mean that an individual can't put something online for a prospective employer. One excellent reason to do so would be if the jobseeker's name comes from a language that may be unfamiliar to a hiring professional.

Many times people are reticent to call or connect when they do not know the gender of an individual. Also, in many instances, there may be concern about language fluency. Some of these concerns can be managed on LinkedIn with a recent picture and some indication of the jobseeker's background. For example, a note on LinkedIn or communication about the position indicating that the applicant grew up in New Hampshire or San Francisco might put a hiring professional's concern to rest. The same goes for someone from the "English-speaking" world who indicates that they grew up and attended schools in Cambodia, Ecuador, Germany, and Japan.

Salvaged phone interview

The recruiter e-mailed Dave to set up an appointment on Monday afternoon. The e-mail requested time on either Tuesday or Wednesday. Dave responded and asked for Wednesday afternoon. The recruiter suggested 2 PM, and Dave agreed. Since he worked as an IT desktop customer services technician and was on the road throughout the day, he made arrangements to be in a quiet place on Wednesday where he could focus and concentrate.

On Tuesday at 2 PM the recruiter called. Dave was in his car on the interstate and didn't know how to respond. He wondered if he had misunderstood. He knew the reception would be spotty at best, and yet he had to get to a client's office by 3 PM. His only option was to take the call and talk on speakerphone.

The recruiter went through Dave's entire résumé, almost line by line, and asked for specific details. David went to his

3 PM client, finished up his workday, and checked his earlier communication with the recruiter. It seemed clear to him that the appointment had been scheduled for Wednesday.

Dave decided to send an e-mail. In it, he thanked the recruiter for his time and apologized for sounding unprepared for the interview. He referenced his understanding that the interview was supposed to be on Wednesday.

The recruiter responded almost immediately with an apology. Another interview was scheduled where Dave was better prepared. Although he didn't get that position, he was able to demonstrate professionalism with the recruiter and request that he be considered for positions that better matched his qualifications.

Regardless of the technology being used, misunderstandings are inevitable. Maintaining an even-tempered emotional state along with a professional demeanor is a highly prized attribute in fast-paced, emotionally charged work environments. Communication challenges are an excellent opportunity to demonstrate these and similar-valued personal characteristics. They will not be overlooked by the hiring communities.

Managing big concerns

Steve graduated with a degree in mechanical engineering. Due to "technology" glitches with the bursar's database at his school, several grades of *F* were not removed from his transcript, even though he retook the classes within the required time frame. Since he had transferred into the school after his junior year, his grade point average only included three semesters of grades.

This left his graduating grade point average at 1.7 out of 4.0. He tried for more than a year to get the grades removed without success. Every job he applied to asked for his grade point average. No matter how he explained the problem, he was unable to get an interview.

We decided on a strategy that utilized a blog, *The International Journal of Mechanical Engineering and Applications,* and his LinkedIn account. Every two weeks, he selected and read an article, wrote a synopsis, checked all the references, and then published it on his personal blog. He then reported his activity on his LinkedIn account. He joined groups with interests related to his blog and occasionally requested that members give him feedback.

Steve increased the number of connections on LinkedIn by watching the activity in his group and connecting with people who had common interests. When he was called for an interview, he printed several of his best blog posts. He found connections who had worked at the interviewing company who coached him on the interview.

Even though he had been out of school for more than two years, and even though there were candidates with master's degrees, he was ready for the hard questions concerning his grades and what he had been doing since he graduated. He got the job!

Here's what he said,

> "Thank you for asking about my grades and the past two years of my life. The grades are the result of a technology issue from school. My professors wrote letters [he had copies with him], but the school has not found a way to resolve the database issues.
>
> "As for the last two years, yes, I've been working in a manufacturing company. I get up at 3 AM every day to be at work on time. I receive a set of blueprints that I have to put together by the time the truck leaves at 2 PM. It's just like being in a research lab. Everything has to be checked and rechecked. If there's a problem and it isn't found, then it has to be redone.
>
> "But it isn't engineering. So I've been reviewing articles in the IJMEA to keep up in the industry and know what is happening. I've been publishing on my blog. Here are some of my favorites."

Attention-getting mechanism for HR

Kasheenah wanted to work for the nonprofit arm of a top US technology corporation. She also wanted to move from Kentucky to Seattle. She had a varied background and had recently worked hard and earned her Project Management Professional Certification.

She filed repeated applications and didn't receive any interest. Kasheenah opened a Twitter account and began following every account that supported the nonprofit organization where she wanted to work. Every time there was a news article or announcement, Kasheenah promoted the article or event. She followed the organization on Facebook and LinkedIn and became a "goodwill machine" where this company was concerned.

Kasheenah recorded her numbers, and her plan is to report her company promotions in the results statements on her résumé.

At the writing of this book, social recruiting is mushrooming as hundreds of recruiters join Twitter. They are finding ways to identify people who are "social savvy" and engaged with their professional communities. In addition, many companies are outsourcing the positions they want filled—not just executives, but even at the entry level.

Everyone who wants to have a consistent income will be wise to watch all aspects of hiring trends, especially where social media are concerned. Many recruiters are immediately available through Twitter and LinkedIn. To ignore them could be an oversight with grave consequences.

Jobsearch toolbox maintenance

The point has been made several times that the skills listed above are not likely going to change significantly, although the tools to manage and demonstrate those skills may change dramatically. Keeping up with trends in the hiring process is a wise investment of time. The next point is that every person who wants to remain employed should think of their toolset as an engine that drives their career. It needs regular attention and maintenance. This will be discussed in greater detail later in the book.

TOOLBOX CREATION, SECTION 1–HARD TOOLS

You may be as tired of reading, "At the writing of this book . . ." as I am of typing it. but the purpose of this book is to produce something that you, the reader, can continue to use as change continues to happen. You may need other sources of information as trends change; however, our intention is that the principles here will allow you to continue to manage your career, regardless of the changes in the economy, your industry, and the implications from the newest technologies.

In this section, we will review those tools that have become standards in the hiring process and others that are newer. All of them may morph into something different, however, the information that they present and the intended audiences will not likely change.

Cover letters and résumés

Most people consider the résumé as the standard-bearer of any jobsearch. Truly it should be the standard-bearer of any career, a living, breathing, dynamic document. Depending on your industry, a curriculum vitae may be required.

Résumé, curriculum vitae, or hybrid?

A résumé is specific to a particular position. It is not a comprehensive document but a selection of relevant information that the jobseeker deems helpful to a hiring professional.

A curriculum vitae (CV) is a comprehensive document of your complete professional history. It may have several appendices that include every professional event, presentation, and conference that you have attended. It will include all articles, journal reviews, and professional citations—everything! These documents are called for and needed by scientific and academic communities. Occasionally, the legal industry and government positions may require a complete curriculum vitae.

Over time the needs of companies have changed. They needed parts of the curriculum vitae but not all of it. For example, a research firm may need a full documentation of a candidate's research activities and his or her publications, but they are not interested in presentations at professional conferences. Consequently, the needs of the company or organization are often given with specific instructions to the potential candidate.

The biggest résumé mistake:

It's an experience, not just information! It's an easy oversight. When people read a résumé, they are *experiencing* the person behind those words. Compare it to starting a relationship.

What is the first thing that people generally want to know about someone when they meet? Is it their educational or professional pedigree? Imagine starting a conversation with, "Hello, my name is Casey. I have an MBA, and I recently passed my PMP Certification." Hmm . . . I understand that résumés have a specific audience with specific needs; I also understand that the audience is under great time constraints. The audience and their needs will set the context on how to proceed. Nonetheless, I have little reason to believe that most jobseekers truly consider their audience. I didn't! This applies to both the cover letter and résumé.

Reader-based cover letters and résumés

This is the big question: Is your cover letter and résumé reader based? If not, then your likelihood of getting an interview has plummeted.

Who are the readers and what do they need to know—and in what order? Here is a partial reader list which may change depending on your industry, new modifications in the technology used in the hiring process, and changes in the hiring process itself. For the foreseeable future, these "players" are not going to change. These are decisions that (not counting number 1 on the list) technology cannot make.

1. The applicant tracking system (ATS)

2. Human Resources professional, Round One. 8–10 seconds

3. Human Resources assistants who call to confirm information they couldn't find on the résumé

4. Human Resources, Round Two. 20-second to 2-minute review

5. Hiring manager

6. Colleagues or potential direct reports

7. The final approver

Each reader has different needs. A clear understanding of each reader's requirement will guide the jobseeker to meet their needs when creating the résumé. This is the document that usually creates the first impression.

The applicant tracking systems (ATS).

Most jobseekers and career coaches know that the ATS will "read" your materials. The system needs keyword-rich information that is context appropriate. The new applicant tracking systems in their third and fourth generation will be GPS-enabled and have contextual capabilities.

There are technologists who have an understanding of search engine optimization (SEO) and attempt to conjure jobseekers to use their services to "SEO" their resume for the applicant tracking systems. This assumes that the ATS keywords are the only variable in getting through the system. This is not true. There are additional elimination rounds that ATSs use that include knockout and demographic questions.

HR Round One: The infamous 8-second review

Most jobseekers believe that if they can get through the ATS then someone will read their résumé. Truly that doesn't happen. When I was working on the Forward Motion process that we now use, I handed cover letters and résumés to numerous HR professionals and watched their eyes to see where they looked first, second, and so forth.

It was a total revelation to find that hiring professionals do not read documents from top to bottom or from left to right. This was a stunning revelation!

In the first pass, in 8 seconds or less HR professionals want to know one thing: Are you qualified for the position? That's it. That information has to be easy to find and process—in 8 seconds or less—period. This information goes on your cover letter. If your cover letter includes narrative of your work history or other information that is found on your résumé, that information is rarely read. This is an 8-second pass. Again, narrative is rarely read.

There are a few exceptions to this rule. In certain nonprofit settings, where the candidate's personal commitment is essential to their success, in those cases, compelling narrative is essential.

Critical Success Factor: Once a candidate is deemed qualified for a position, the cover letter is usually eliminated. Therefore anything that is important to your qualifications for the position must also be on the résumé.

HR assistants: The paperwork screening and/or phone call

When applicants get through the ATS and pass the 8-second review, they may receive a phone call from an HR assistant.

The purpose is simple: they want to be sure you *qualify* for the position.

In other words, your materials passed five ATS filters and the 8-second test. When the HR assistant looks at your materials, they should find the information that indicates you qualify for the position. If not, you may receive a 10-to-15-minute call to verify that information. *This call is not an interview.*

It is likely that you will be checked out online, and your LinkedIn profile should confirm the basic content in your cover letter and résumé. If you don't have a LinkedIn profile with substance, then you may be eliminated at this juncture.

Viable recommendations from colleagues, managers, and supervisors are important. Many recruiters will not consider someone who doesn't have any recommendations for past work on their LinkedIn profile. Further, when jobseekers have not given recommendations to their co-workers, this raises concern they may not get along well in the workplace.

HR 20-second to 2-minute review

At this point, your cover letter and résumé has to give the hiring professional a solid reason to pick up the phone. Four questions they are looking for include:

1. Is there evidence that you will enjoy this position? (E.g., this position falls into your chosen career path, that it is a logical next step.)

2. Do you have the core competencies and attributes that will make you a good fit for the position as well as the company?

3. What makes you unique? This is the place and time for your Unique Value Statement (UVS). It should be on your cover letter and résumé! What is unique about you? What makes you stand out from the rest of the candidates? (This critical success factor will be discussed at length in the next section.)

4. If you are still in the running, then the final question comes up: Is the work history on your résumé something HR can send to a hiring manager who can assess your ability to do the job?

   This is where your job activities and functions, results statements and your ability to positively contribute to an environment or work culture should clearly be evident.

Critical Success Factor: The response to these four questions should be easily found—at a glance.

The "quick-read" by the hiring manager

Hiring managers have three primary concerns:

1. Can you do the job?

2. How long will you take to get up to speed? (How much hand-holding will you need?)

3. Will your interactions with the team be positive and encourage productivity, or will they create unnecessary tension?

Your résumé should give insights into these questions in the details of your work history.

The final approver

It will never cease to amaze me that the final approver may spend more time with your résumé than anyone else in the process. But after all, this is the person who approves the budget allocation for the position.

This person wants to know if you have been thoroughly vetted. Is your "pedigree" in place? Do you have a history of successful work integration? Will you represent the company well and contribute to the overall mission with a sense of urgency and ownership?

Contract negotiations

If you are offered a job, your résumé will be used to determine the specifics of your job offer. Once again, it is critical that the details are in place. Your résumé, especially, sets the foundation for your final contract. Your document becomes the basis for the legal contract that will bind you with your future employer.

Time-honored essential guidelines for cover letters and résumés

Although the cover letter and résumé may change in what it is called or how it is delivered, there are some essential characteristics that are not going to change.

Formality and polish

While the word *résumé* is still used, it is a formal document. It should be given the utmost polish. Some people believe that the word résumé (with accents) is dated. My personal opinion is that it isn't about being dated. Instead, it is a matter of formality. It's like the "formal event" that commands a tuxedo or formal evening dress.

This initial presentation is the opportunity to make a statement to the reader that the position is important to you and you have carefully considered every detail as a demonstration of who you are at your core.

That said, with every detail in place, you are well positioned to negotiate the best possible contract to receive the compensation you deserve.

It's all about them

One of the biggest surprises that surfaced in interviews with countless hiring professionals (HR, managers, recruiters, etc.) was their distaste for *Summary* sections, *Objective* statements, and *Overview* sections. I didn't understand their aversion. It seemed that those sections could quickly save them time.

The problem is that these sections are all about the jobseeker. It is logical that if a jobseeker is presenting himself or herself, the communication is focused on them. But astute jobseekers know that it isn't about them. Instead, it is about their ability to understand the pain of the potential employer and show how they can relieve that pain.

Critical Success Factor: Objective and summary statements are all about the jobseeker, not the need of the potential employer. The employer's "pain" can be found on the job posting. They are in pain, and they believe that if someone can do what is described on that posting, it will relieve their pain.

This is a new concept for some jobseekers, even now in 2016. An example of this will follow.

Top critical success factor: Differentiation

An individual's Unique Value Statement (UVS) is a critical success factor. Most people that apply for a position can probably do the job—at least they believe they can. So discussing what is already evident (skills, education, experience) is not going to differentiate the jobseeker from the pack.

One of the first questions that jobseekers can expect in interviews and networking situations is the inquiry, "Please tell me about yourself." Most jobseekers today start with the usual information that is on their résumé. You know the stuff: "I have a bachelor's degree in _____ and over twenty years of experience in _____."

The answer to "Tell me about yourself" has to be placed on the résumé even before the question ever gets asked in an interview. Usually it shows up in that section entitled *Objective*, *Overview*, or *Summary*. I am certain that the jobseeker intends to give some kind of synopsis of their history. They are trying to save the hiring professional time! Bad news: it backfires. It has been used for decades, and still, most jobseekers hold on to this section of their résumé. As mentioned in the previous section, we believe there is something better.

Forward Motion coined the term *Organizational Value* to replace the jobseeker-centered objective statement. In this brief, not more than three-line statement, we specify top attributes and contributions of the jobseeker that will help a company or organization solve the need expressed in the job posting. It is the jobseeker's Unique Value Statement. It isn't about skill sets, pedigree, or experience. It's about who they are as an individual that will help the company solve their pain problem and meet their goals.

The Unique Value Statement should incorporate three key elements:

1. Attributes of the candidate

2. The goals, vision, or mission of the organization

3. The problem the candidate will solve

Here are a few examples of an Organizational Value that integrates the candidate's UVS:

- My ability to build trusting relationships and create unique, yet practical programs will support the clients, build business value, and grow the market share for _____ (organization name).

- My ability to support the long-term goals through practical, safety-focused manufacturing practices and deliver projects on time and within budget will earn client trust and build loyalty for _____ (organization name).

- My ability to administer and build programs; attract, recruit, and select exceptional talent; and develop supportive collegial relationships will support and augment the goals of _____ (organization name).

Top critical success factor: One comprehensive message

Most jobseekers extend the length of their jobsearch by loading their résumé with every conceivable activity for every job they have held. As explained earlier, unless they are creating a curriculum vitae, every jobseeker should have a customizable résumé that highlights their unique value and supports their statement that describes how they will be able to solve the potential employer's pain. It is one comprehensive message.

A candidate's UVS message should be found on LinkedIn, as well as in every answer that the jobseeker responds to in an interview. Everything that goes on the cover letter and résumé, and every communication with the potential hiring entity should contribute to this message. This even applies to everything the jobseeker says during the interview process.

Top critical success factor: Manage any concerns in the moment

Since the Unique Value Statement is the core message that a jobseeker must communicate and since everything else should support that message, it becomes evident that there will be "issues" that have to be addressed.

One of the most common is a gap in employment. This tends to unnerve many jobseekers. However, it should be mentioned that in the first five years of the Great Recession, 20 percent of American workers were laid off. *http://www.latimes.com/business/la-fi-layoffs-unemployment-jobs-economy-20140924-story.html* So an employment gap isn't really new or unusual. But it does need to be addressed.

Sometimes the solution is simple. For example, a person returned to school full-time to complete a master's degree. Another common situation includes a "boomer" who was laid off, resigned, or accepted a demotion to take care of an elderly parent.

Everyone has "issues." The point is that they have to be managed right when the reader reads the concern. Once the concern surfaces, if it isn't addressed, then the candidate may be eliminated from consideration.

Case study: Career switch

Jeanette was a scientist, and after eleven successful years in laboratories, she decided that she was ready for a change. She entered the field of scientific instrument sales. It was a logical move since she understood the scientific communities and their work environment. After six successful years, she had moved into national accounts and led a team of five sales reps. She was excellent with the team, found meaningful incentive programs and their performance was stellar. Jeanette travelled over 80 percent of the time—which she enjoyed and considered a perk.

When her father became ill, Jeanette knew her mother would not be able to manage the situation. There was no way to manage her job and give her parents the support they needed. Jeanette resigned to help her parents.

During the time that her father's health deteriorated, Jeanette's mother also became ill. As Jeanette assessed her situation, she realized that what she thought would be short hiatus from her profession was going to take at least two or three years.

She became licensed as a real estate agent and began to build an income. The position gave her the flexibility she needed to care for her parents, and she remained in a sales environment, connecting with people and keeping her skills sharp.

Five years later, Jeanette was ready to return to her former career in scientific sales. This break in continuity had to be managed on her résumé to the satisfaction of recruiters. After several attempts, and with feedback from hiring profession-als, Jeanette put the following statement under her real estate experience:

> *Interim work while attending to the health needs of a family member.*

That's all it took. Readers understood the situation and correctly assumed that the matter was resolved.

The danger of too much information

- If a mid-career jobseeker puts *everything* on their résumé, why would the hiring professional need to call?

- If we disclose everything about us on a résumé, eventually, there will be something that takes us out of the running. The same goes for interviews. A quick rule of thumb is "Keep talking and you will give them a reason not to hire you."
- Hiring professionals need the information that is relevant. Being selective with what is disclosed is appreciated.

Case study: Poor "issue" management

Glenn was in his late forties and had been laid off from a global manufacturing company. He had senior executive experience and expertise in global operations, supply chain, and project management. His résumé showed a promotion every two or three years.

His experience with people management was highly successful. His education and certifications were all in place. His results statements were spectacular. Although the layoff was a shock, Glenn was confident that with his extensive global experience, his stellar accomplishments, and his proven track record, he would soon find a job.

Unfortunately, when Glenn was laid off, large manufacturing companies were cutting back. He insisted on creating a comprehensive résumé (seven pages) that demonstrated in great detail that his skill sets were flexible and he could function in a variety of roles. He emphasized his global experience, especially the Asian markets.

A few recruiters called and asked Glenn what he *really* wanted to do. With the ability and experience to manage any one of three directions, there was consistent concern that he didn't have a preference and would take any job that was offered—and that he would leave if something better surfaced.

The recruiters were also concerned that with Glenn's background in a large company, a midsized company wouldn't have enough challenge. The cost of bringing in a C-Suite executive that stayed for only a year or two was a risk that companies were unwilling to take.

Glenn traveled around the United States to one interview after another. He repeatedly asked for feedback. Repeatedly he was told that his background looked incredible. He seemed too good to be true. He was overqualified. After over twelve interviews in two years, an offer never came.

Solution: Glenn might have first prioritized his jobsearch according to the market. If he wanted to stay with large corporations, then project management, at that time, would have likely been his best choice. His résumé would then have only the support for project management. If he was more interested in a C-Suite position, then he would have had to manage the concern. So his LinkedIn profile and his résumé might have included a context statement to the point:

> *Although most of my experience has been in large, global manufacturing corporations, I have been watching the trends in my industry, and I am enthusiastic to see that smaller, more flexible companies are growing and gaining market share. My hope is to find a position*

in such a company where my skill sets can be put to the greatest advantage.

Recruiters called Glenn and repeatedly asked about the salary. Smaller companies would not be able to pay his former salary. Again, Glenn failed to manage their concern. The simple solution would have been to reiterate the context statement and then assure the recruiter that in the two years since he had been laid off, he had adjusted his finances, and the market value at a smaller company would work nicely.

LinkedIn profile

As we have already discussed, the importance of a business-social presence as part of career management has steadily grown, and we believe that social assets are a critical success factor for having and keeping employment. The role of the LinkedIn profile in the jobsearch is varied; however, I believe that it can serve as a personable (not personal) outreach to potential employers.

As discussed, the résumé should be a polished, formal document. We know that over 94 percent of hiring professionals check a potential candidate's LinkedIn profile when they decide whether to call. That makes the LinkedIn profile a perfect middle ground between the formal document and the phone call. The document is formal; the call is personal. A personable LinkedIn profile is the perfect "middle voice" in the process.

This means that the profile section is a perfect opportunity to present a professional image with a personal, approachable tone. I encourage jobseekers to write three paragraphs, where they essentially talk to their readers.

The first paragraph discusses what the jobseeker finds exciting and what they most enjoy from a professional perspective. The second paragraph gives a brief overview of the challenges that the jobseeker sees in their industry and how they uniquely bring solutions (the UVS!) These should be given in a positive, professional tone. Finally, the third paragraph gives insights into industry challenges and how they may be met.

This may sound daunting to some people, but it doesn't have to be. Simply "talk" to your reader.

In the experience section, I recommend that the career manager write a brief narrative that highlights key successes, followed by a brief set of bullets that outline key results.

There are positions that allow the jobseeker to auto-apply for a job by allowing the ATS to access information from the jobseeker's LinkedIn profile.

This assumes that the jobseeker's profile is essentially the same information as the résumé which would prohibit any kind of customization or selection of pertinent information for the position. Another concern is that LinkedIn is a business social site. When jobseekers' LinkedIn profiles carry the content of their entire résumé, then the opportunity is lost to be "social"!

Also there is no way that the LinkedIn profile can present the information about a jobseeker with the quality of excellence and the degree of polish that a résumé brings to the reader.

Finally, current practices change. Keep up with what is new and the trends in presenting yourself on all social platforms.

Networking tool: Professional bio

Networking is imperative for effective career management and will be discussed in the next section. For jobseekers, especially executives, it can become awkward to follow-up after a meeting by sending a résumé. Earlier in the book, it was noted that one of the biggest mistakes jobseekers make is miseducating their network. The way to avoid this is with a professional bio.

This one-page document should include the following:

- Career mission

- Career highlights

- Notable (selected) accomplishments

- Strengths and leadership style

- Influencers

- Affiliations

- Education

- Short quotes from recommenders

This information should be sent to a graphic designer with a high-resolution professional image and tastefully arranged as a one-page printable document. It should also be available as a PDF.

During a networking event, the bio can be offered as a springboard for conversation. Following a networking meeting (phone, e-mail, face-to-face . . . whatever), a jobseeker can send a thank-you note via e-mail and attach the bio. If their contact decides to extend an introduction, then they have a professional document to accompany the contact. Likewise, when someone asks for information, the professional bio can serve to educate the interested party and present a professional image with accurate messaging in place.

TOOLBOX CREATION, SECTION 2–SOFT TOOLS

The first section of Part Four of this book deals with the hard tools, meaning those aspects of the jobsearch that include consistent documentation that quickly and clearly explains information about the jobseeker and how s/he can bring benefit to an organization.

This section of Part Four focuses on the soft tools, meaning those aspects of the jobsearch that are delivered in person. This includes every phone conversation and networking meeting, even discussions at support groups. It also includes casual written "conversation" such as e-mails, responses on LinkedIn, chatrooms, and so forth.

Many jobseekers think that "interviewing" means talking about themselves. It's understandable that so many people find that distasteful and the discomfort isn't unusual. The good news is that interviewing isn't about the jobseeker as much as one might think. Interviews, *all* interviews, should accomplish two things:

1. The jobseeker should gain a deeper understanding about the position and the company. Even in a networking appointment, questions should be asked that give the jobseeker or candidate a deeper understanding of the situation, the challenges that are faced, and the general stress that a company is facing.

2. The company should gain a deeper understanding about the jobseeker's character and professional demeanor and get a sense that they will or will not fit into the culture. If the appointment has no particular job to fill, such as a networking meeting, then the conversation should focus on the industry and the company's challenges and how the jobseeker or candidate can help.

This philosophy mandates an unusual approach from both the jobseeker and interviewer. True networking is finding ways where both parties are mutually better for having met.

Most people don't like to focus on themselves, but most people do enjoy finding ways to help someone else. This, in my opinion, is the point of every interview.

Time-honored essentials for the interview process

As with the written set of tools, every person who needs or wants a consistent revenue stream will need a single comprehensive message, their UVS, that is the foundational content for their communications. Any deviation from the core message should be carefully thought through to ensure it doesn't raise any concerns or give a mixed message to the listener.

Regardless of the situation or whether the appointment is a networking meeting or a final interview for the job of your dreams, your job is to prepare your audience to answer two questions:

1. Who should I (we) hire? And . . .

2. Why should I (we) hire you?

At the end of a networking meeting the questions are similar:

1. How can I utilize you? Or . . . Who do I know that I can introduce you to?

2. Why should I do so?

The answer to these two questions should be evident:

1. They should hire YOU! Or suggest you to someone they want you to help.

2. They know and can articulate your Unique Value. I.e. "I want to hire Jim because he understands the big picture, and his relationship-building skills will build the trust and loyalty we need with our customers to raise our profit margins . . . and he seems practical as well. I like that."

Keep to the script!

This book has spent enormous time and space to help the jobseeker understand his or her Unique Value. This is the central message that permeates every written word—and now every spoken word as well.

The UVS is the script. Reader, if you haven't scripted your UVS, this is the time to do it! Here is mine:

I have the ability to identify unique solutions that solve complex problems and then develop practical, memorable training programs that teach people long-term career management.

If I wanted something more generic, which could be applied to *any* company or organization, it might read:

I have the ability to identify unique solutions that solve complex problems and then develop practical, memorable programs to assist [employees, students, companies] to meet their long-term goals.

The point here is that the statement can be adapted for any situation. It's about finding solutions and relieving pain. The statement expresses how I work, what I do, and the end-results. The situation doesn't matter. I can apply my UVS to any problem.

It's *always* about their pain

All of career management could be summed up in these words: "Where perceived pain meets perceived need—someone will be hired." From the jobseeker's perspective, the goal is a continuous, personal revenue stream. Ensuring that continuous income is all about understanding the perceived pain within an organization and the perceived need. This is the research that jobseekers should undertake to manage their careers. They must know their industry and be able to clearly state how they will relieve the pain (their UVS!).

If you need a job, a better job . . . go look for the pain element in an organization. Ask all sorts of questions about this pain. Understand it from a global industry perspective, from the company perspective, from within the business unit, and especially from the perspective of the manager or supervisor. Then apply your UVS!

Different audiences have different pain. As you have discussions with various people, you will develop a deeper understanding of what kinds of messages are needed and the language that best resonates with their needs. Some observations are included here from past experience with members in the hiring process, each of whom has specific needs.

Human Resource professionals and recruiters

Human Resource professionals are looking for people that will contribute to the environment without stressing it. This is part of their quest for "cultural fit." Their questions will reflect their concerns.

Example:

> HR: "How would your colleagues describe you?"
>
> Candidate A: "They know that I'm the person who can get the job done. I'm dependable and reliable. I'm the person that does whatever it takes."

Candidate B: "They know that no matter what, they can come to me and I will listen carefully. Together we will identify a solution, and they know I'll check back with them and follow up."

Although the first answer is valid, HR knows that Candidate A stresses the environment. Candidate B keeps the workplace focused and productive.

Carefully listen to questions from the Human Resource professionals and recruiters, and understand what is behind the questions. This question wasn't about loyalty, reliability, or determination. It was about interactions in the workplace and how the candidate manages himself or herself.

Managers and supervisors

Managers tend to ask questions that focus on whether the person can do the job and their general demeanor while on the job. Managers generally want to know the following:

- How long will this person take to add value?
- How much handholding will they need?
- Will they get along with the rest of the team?

Senior executives

This can be a bit tricky. In general, executives want to know what it is like to have you in their space. They may tell you stories and not really ask any questions. They are under considerable pressure, and having an employee who adds to that isn't helpful. The message that most executives need to hear is:

> *"You can count on me to be forthright about issues or concerns. If there is a problem, I'll be sure that you are aware of it, and I'll have ideas on potential resolutions. I understand that people in your position generally don't like surprises."*

Support the script: Apply your UVS

Every professional conversation and every interview will require the jobseeker to support his or her UVS with some kind of documentation. The résumé should include Experience Details and Results statements. Those are factual but not personal. The information on the résumé doesn't have the emotional context that brings personal meaning.

To support their UVS, every jobseeker should have three or four carefully crafted stories that demonstrate the value they brought to a situation. Stories have been proven to increase the impression left by the person who tells them. This is crucial, since hiring practices limit the time spent with candidates, and the field of candidates has increased to five on average. Consequently, telling a compelling, well-crafted story can contribute to being memorable and getting an offer.

Behavioral interviews

These demonstrations of past successes will likely be used during the behavioral interview. This process has now been adapted by most companies.

The hiring community (in about 2011) determined that past performance is one of the best predictors of future performance. According to the University of Delaware, "behavioral interviewing is said to be 55 percent predictive of future on-the-job behavior, while traditional interviewing is only 10 percent predictive." *https://c.ymcdn.com/sites/www.acpm.org/resource/resmgr/careers-files/behav_interview.pdf*

Behavioral interviewing has become the norm, and short of an on-the-job-trial, this approach will not likely go away. Behavioral interviewing questions are simply those that ask the candidate about their past. There are two types of questions:

1. Tell me about a time when . . .

2. What would you do if . . . ?

This is when the candidate should be ready with stories of their past that clearly demonstrate their UVS. There are several standard "templates" for answering behavioral questions. They all follow the same principles.

STAR method:	SAR method	PAR method
• S–Situation (set the stage) • T–Task (your goal) • A–Action (what you did) • R–Result (the end state)	• S–Situation • A–Action (what you did) • R–Result (the end state)	• P–Problem • A–Action (what you did) • R–Result (the end state)

I personally believe that they fall short of one important point. These methods leave out the important information regarding how a person thought through the situation. They do not give the listener any idea of the considerations involved in the decision to determine the action.

As an extension of the PAR method, I have adapted it to PAAR:

- P–Problem (pain)
- A–Analysis (what did you think? your considerations)
- A–Action (what you did)
- R–Result (the end state, *or* what people said)

There is substantial information on the Internet regarding the first three methods or approaches to responding to behavioral questions.

Consider the following points:

- Use only two sentences for each point.
- The entire story should take less than two minutes.
- The story should end with a question to the listener to ensure it responded to the interviewer's concern. I.e.: "Is there anything there you would like me to elaborate on?" The reason behind this is that most people spend too much time on the situation or task, rather than focusing on the action and result.

To be effective, these stories should be crafted and practiced until the points can be communicated in a natural manner. They should not sound scripted.

Manage your enthusiasm

When we are communicating in person, whether by Skype or telephone or in person, this is when our interest and enjoyment come through. The word *passion* has been overused and is more than a bit uncomfortable for many people. Too much enthusiasm, and a candidate can be dismissed. Too little energy, and there is a sense of disinterest.

My preference is to give a sense of urgency without negative intensity. Suggestion: Match the level of intensity/energy/enthusiasm of the person conducting the interview, plus a little bit.

Close the interview/conversation

The last few moments of a conversation are critical, regardless of whether it's a networking or formal interview. This is the time to review what you have learned and reiterate your UVS. It's the last thought that you want to leave with your listener.

There are three components to the closing statement:

- Brief review
- Your UVS
- Next steps

Here is an example of a closing statement:

> *"Thank you for your time. I have a much better idea of [the company, the position, your challenges . . .]. What I believe I can bring to the situation is my [insert*

UVS: ability to build relationships, develop practical solutions that will support the strategic goals of the organization . . .]. What are the next steps?" (This refers to the hiring process or someone's assistance by introducing you to a colleague or associate.)

Additional considerations when speaking to others

- Again: remember that a company would not interview anyone unless they believed they could already do the job. Therefore, they are more interested in who you are and your professional demeanor than in what you can do. All of that is on the résumé.

- Less is more. I often remind people that the more they say, the more likely they will raise a concern with a potential employer.

Virtual (online) conversations and "social media"

Every e-mail and voicemail, any communication or touch point, should be pleasant, professional, and without *any* emotional baggage.

Social media accounts often surface during a jobsearch. Every jobseeker (employed or not) should routinely check their online presence. This includes variations of a person's name, with and without initials. Although *you* may not have done anything, remember that social media have brought us together as a global community. There is a strong likelihood that someone else having your name, or a variation of it, may have "digital dirt" associated with you.

If you have social media accounts, the rule applies: pleasant and professional. There can be no exceptions to this. Social recruiting is mushrooming, and the hiring communities are looking into every dimension of a person's profile to find the best possible match.

Caveat

The discussion here is not offered as a comprehensive guide to interviewing or networking. Rather, it is meant to present the most overlooked aspects of verbal presentation of your unique value and how to express it. This section is intended to identify principles of communication that will help the careful jobseeker to successfully manage his or her career.

STEPS TO IMPLEMENT YOUR STRATEGY

What good is a strategy without a plan to implement it? The best strategy in the world is of no use whatsoever, if the implementation is poor or mediocre. Therefore, Part Five is one of the most important parts of the book. There are several components to a career strategy, all of which contribute to the continued success and goal of earning a steady income. Each of these components are discussed in this section.

The role of recruiters

Recruiters play a critical role in the global jobs crisis. Yet they are frequently criticized by jobseekers, who often misunderstand what recruiters do and how they do it. They are businesses, and they cannot change the world they work in; all they can do is respond to it. And in a world where the Internet means that any and every job advertised receives dozens or even hundreds of applications, how recruiters select suitable candidates has also had to change.

Yet recruiters consistently report that the majority of jobseekers have unrealistic expectations of them and, worse, do little to ensure they interact with recruiters in a way that maximizes their chances of passing screening, let alone being shortlisted. To discover the truth, we asked Jorg Stegemann, CEO of Kennedy Executive, to provide his insights into this topic. Kennedy Executive makes executive placements in all sectors in the global job market.

Q: What do we need to know about the recruitment business?

Jorg Stegemann: "You do not need a certificate or diploma to work in this business, and anyone with a phone and business cards can set up a recruitment business within a couple of days." And this is what happens in boom times. The crisis of 2001 cleaned up the market and threw many (mostly small) recruitment firms out of business; the crisis of 2008 then killed many smaller but also some of the big recruitment firms. Today, the recruitment industry is fragmented.

"In general, in crisis or boom times, jobseekers have to bear in mind that it's not the candidate but the hiring company that is our client and pays the bill. Candidates say we are bad people who run after the money because we do not meet them when they are seeking a job. The reality is that if I met every candidate who wants to meet me, I would be in interviews all the time without having time to search jobs, and as a consequence, I would go out of business in nine months' time.

"Jobseekers may look at recruiters as a 'ray of hope,' the light in the dark universe. They see recruiters as gatekeepers to their future—a recruiter is a hub of potential jobs, jobs they can't access. They don't seem to realize that recruiters are looking out for their clients—not the jobseeker. There's a mismatch of expectations on both sides. But then candidates should not expect too much: statistics say that the chance you find your next job through a recruiter is 15 percent (5 percent job ad and 80 percent network)."

Takeaway for jobseekers: This is how you should think and act. Otherwise it will trip you up. Recruiters are really busy. A recruiter's goal is to maximize revenue for their firm. They will take the shortest and easiest route to do that. So jobseekers should come with a complete portfolio—ready to be presented to the recruiter's client. Recruiters are frustrated: they are often presented with jobseekers in the raw. They aren't ready or "packaged" in the way the recruiter wants.

Recruiters are drowning with too much information to digest. Yet few candidates present themselves to recruiters with their application clear enough for recruiters to present them to their clients.

Jorg Stegemann: "Yes, speed of execution is important, but my best tip for a candidate would rather be to return calls and provide missing information faster than your 'competitors' (i.e., the other candidates). However, I reject the very common standpoint that recruiters 'do not bend over for jobseekers.' Many in the industry treat candidates badly and clients well—without thinking of the fact that this changes all the time: clients become candidates and candidates become clients. This is why I do not categorize people as 'candidates' and 'clients.' They are all 'contacts.' What is the real difference between a 'candidate' and a 'client'? They are all people—it's just that some of them are currently looking for a new job.

"LinkedIn profiles are critical. A weak or sketchy profile may eliminate a candidate before anyone even looks at their résumé. Jobseekers place too much faith in job-boards and ads and don't pay enough attention to building relationships with the right recruiters. When I ask jobseekers how they are approaching the market, nine out of ten are saying, 'I am sending applications.' This is not enough. To find a new job, a variety of techniques must be applied: network first of all, at conferences, on LinkedIn, at job fairs and with two or three headhunters you trust and who will counsel you on the salary, the interview, and the strategic career choices you have to make.

"According to CBS [a UK recruitment firm: *http://www .cbsrecruitment.co.uk/*], 98 percent of all (internal or external) recruiters look their candidates up on Google. Whilst there are still professions that make less use of LinkedIn (doctors, architects etc.), it is the platform to be present on for most corporate jobs. LinkedIn is you.com. A bad presence on Linkedin can eliminate a candidate even before the interview. After all, LinkedIn is how you present yourself; it is accessible 24/7 and in theory to 7 billion people. So you'd better make sure it is good."

Jorg Stegemann: "The top Linkedin mistakes I see are: 1) unprofessional picture; 2) long-winded, unclear, or superficial presentation of the jobs; and 3) sloppiness such as typos, wrong dates, and outdated contact data."

Jorg Stegemann: "Your LinkedIn profile is the first work your future employer sees from you. On viewing a sloppy profile, their conclusion is if a candidate's self-presentation is sloppy, how will the candidate represent the company's product or service?"

Q: Will online and social media ultimately make recruiters obsolete?

Jorg Stegemann: "Online cannot make recruiters redundant [obsolete] except possibly for low-value high-volume jobs. However, online is changing the business models that recruiters use, and therefore jobseekers have to adapt to these new models.

"The industry will evolve and the best ones will stay. The recruitment industry is currently challenged, yet I believe the future will be bright for the best recruiters i.e. those able (and not too arrogant) to adapt.

"Yes, social media has changed the way we do business today, how we get the information we need to get the work done, and of course how we connect with people. As recruitment stands at the heart of the labor market, we are among the first ones to be impacted by technological or economic changes. Will LinkedIn smash us away and destroy an industry that generates US$400 billion per year worldwide? I do not think so, and the same fear came up when Monster entered the marketplace.

"But like all other industries, recruitment has to reinvent itself. Many jobs can be sourced internally. For middle and upper management, however, it always has been and will be difficult to find the right talent. Recruitment firms have to add value that goes beyond pure recruitment. HR consulting, assessment, coaching, onboarding, outplacement (at Kennedy Exec, we do the latter two), or other services diversify and enrich the offer. Almost all big firms have understood this and diversified their business."

Q: How has the rise of LinkedIn affected recruiters?

Jorg Stegemann: "Is it really useful to recruiters? LinkedIn is presented to users as a networking platform. But their business model is a recruiter platform.

"Ninety-nine percent of all recruiters are on LinkedIn (and the remaining 1 percent are dinosaurs). But there are two different ways recruiters talk about it: the first group denies sourcing candidates here for fear that clients will think, 'Oh, I can do that myself,' and would rather say—but only when asked using the word LinkedIn—'Well, yes, okay, we *also* use LinkedIn—but only a little.' The other ones say openly that LinkedIn helps them to do the business and makes it faster.

"Information is omnipresent. Whether you want to buy a dishwasher in Zurich or hire a marketing manager in New York City, the Internet can help you. But then, how do you cluster the information? Try it out: The search 'Marketing Manager New York City' on LinkedIn gives 48,000 results.

So what should you do? Send 48,000 invitations to a job interview or 48,000 work contracts? Information as such is useless. It is accessible to everyone, and 7 billion people in the world can have the same information on LinkedIn. What you make out of it will make the difference.

"Years and often decades of talking to decision makers, of understanding how companies, industries, and economies tick, of learning and committing errors, of experience and gut feeling are what you pay for when giving your search to a headhunter. I may be wrong, but I feel this cannot be replaced by mathematical algorithms such as the ones LinkedIn (my second best friend, by the way!) is using."

Q: How have your clients' requirements been changing recently?

Jorg Stegemann: "Clients contact us when everything else fails. Middle management jobs are filled mostly internally only, and it appears that the lower end of the market (temp staffing and entry level—we do neither at Kennedy Executive) and the upper segment (this is where we are positioned) remain. Clients have become picky. I hear from some regions in Europe and in the US that it has become more difficult to sell retainers than it used to. Clients compare more, and as the barriers of exit (working today with recruiter A and tomorrow with recruiter B) are zero, loyalty has decreased too."

Q: How do recruiters actually find the people they seek?

Jorg Stegemann: "We sell our clients the skill (or gift?) to find the best talent (for them) in the market. Not only the active but also the passive jobseekers. [A passive candidate is working and not actively looking for a new job.] And there are those who do not seek at all and who might be invisible to the client.

"We start with a target list of companies that are interesting to our clients. Then we identify the right candidates and approach them. This gives the longlist. We then dig deeper, investigate, talk, meet and interview, and ref check the most promising candidates. The end result of all this is the 'shortlist': the three to five best candidates we believe in. This is the fruit of weeks of work and 100 to 150 potentially interesting candidates in the market. A perfect shortlist will present candidates who come from different sources: recommendation (the best ones), direct approach, network (some call it 'database') and yes, of course LinkedIn and sometimes even job ads."

Q: What are the key factors that recruiters look for when they find a jobseeker they want to talk to?

Jorg Stegemann "Respect, responsiveness, honesty, and commitment to go to the end and sign the contract if the job is right."

Q: How can a jobseeker make themselves most attractive to a recruiter?

Jorg Stegemann: "Headhunters have what jobseekers don't have: inside information about your next employer and jobs that will never be advertised. We are watching the job market just like jobseekers, but the difference is that we do nothing else but this, 50 hours per week and 52 weeks per year. And when we find vacancies, our job is to put the right candidate in front of our client. What can jobseekers do to be chosen?"

Jorg Stegemann to jobseekers: Jorg's 7 tips on how to get headhunted:

1. **Get ready:** Do you have the right skills to make a difference? Be critical and realistic yet ambitious with yourself. If you lack a skill or a degree, go and get it. There are good executive education programs out there. Rule of thumb: if you did your last meaningful training longer than ten years ago, take one. Do not only consider what you will learn but also the message it sends on your LinkedIn profile and résumé. Example: an online course on Feng Shui versus "Leading Change and Organizational Renewal" at Harvard Business School. You cannot afford Harvard Business School? Have a look at Coursera, and take for instance "Organizational Analysis" at Stanford or "Corporate Finance" at Wharton—for free

2. **Step out of the shade and become visible:** In order to be found, you must be visible—online and offline. Critical to online visibility are a watertight LinkedIn profile, Twitter, guest posts, or publications. However, you cannot send a handshake by e-mail, and it is hard to build rapport online only. When did you last participate in a networking event? Find circles that interest you such as business, alumni, sports, or other associations. Mingle and make sure you bring enough business cards. Headhunters will always be there too, and your objective is to get on their radar screen.

3. **Be meaningful:** Being visible is good, being meaningful is better. If the last point is the car, this one is the gas to get it moving. This part is about your personal branding, your marketing strategy, or, if you want: your sales plan. Going to conferences is fine, but you will make a real impact by raising questions during the Q&A part. [Jorg suggests asking a relevant question that doesn't challenge so much as draw attention to your understanding and depth.] And if you do so, I guarantee there will be at least three people that will approach you in the coffee break and talk to you about your contribution.

   Online, being meaningful is about sharing content on LinkedIn or Twitter or writing guest posts. LinkedIn discussion forums and updates are a very powerful means to communicate what matters to you and to position you as someone who has something to say. What do you want to be associated with? The information I share is usually on career management, the objective being that people think, "Oh, an update from Jorg. Must be on career management."

4. **Be an expert:** What is your expertise? Let's say it is . . . step dance: your aim should be to become known as the best step-dancer in your market. Establish yourself as an authority by communicating (online and offline as outlined above) about what

you know best to ensure that your name comes up when a headhunter asks one of your contacts, "Who is the best step-dancer in your network?"

5. **"If we don't call you, call us":** Who are the three specialized head hunters for your expertise or niche in your city? Which are the top tier recruitment firms are the most likely to find you a job if you needed one? If you don't have the answer right now, conduct an Internet search. Contact us [recruiters] in an intelligent way (catchy LinkedIn invitation, a recommendation, or a line prior to an industry event that interests us both (e.g., "Jorg, we share an interest in coaching. Might we meet Friday at the XYZ conference?").

6. **How to get headhunted:** Once we are in contact, do not see headhunters in a binary way ("Jorg's only reason to exist is to find me a new job"). Follow the basic rules of networking, and give first, ask second. Share industry information, give us leads, recommend us, send us a relevant article on our sector or our profession. I remember the candidates better who refer me to new, interesting contacts than those I meet once, after which no one follows up . . .

7. **Be good:** If you are not nice, fair, and pleasant, people won't like you. If people don't like you, they will neither think of you nor recommend you. This was an easy one, right?

Jorg Stegemann: "There are no guarantees for anyone to get headhunted, but these seven steps tell you a) how to get visible, b) how to be meaningful, and c) what to do with recruiters once we are in contact. Be strategic, but most importantly authentic and honest, and we can be a catalyst for your career."

Q: With the changes in periods of unemployment, what is a recruiter's view about someone who has been unemployed for 3 months, 6 months, 12 months, or more?

Jorg Stegemann: "This is difficult. I would personally say that 3 months are no problem at all. At a certain level it is normal to negotiate a departure and then look for a new job rather than find it first and resign from your old job second. However, at some point of time, you have to show you have remained active."

Q: What about when a jobseeker has had short bouts of employment (consulting projects, etc.)? Does their value go down?

Jorg Stegemann: "Hard to say. For some managers, it does (my assumption is that this mainly concerns hiring managers who have twenty or so years of tenure and just cannot understand how one can lose your job anyway . . .). Dynamic changes are important and careers are not linear in the 21st century. Sometimes, it gets a little bumpy, and most of us [recruiters] have experienced it ourselves.

"The CV [curriculum vitae or résumé] has several purposes, and one is to predict the future based on the past. Short bouts of employment may be bad luck, opportunity—or the sign that the candidate is not able to perform in a stable way, does not master stress well, or runs away when it gets difficult. A hiring manager on the other side who is looking for someone who will stay for the coming years might draw exactly these conclusions—and refrain from going further."

Q: How should a jobseeker choose which recruiters they approach?

Jorg Stegemann: "While it is almost impossible to recognize a good dentist, it is possible to recognize a good recruiter."

Three triple "x" questions to recognize a good headhunter . . . and help you understand if the recruiter in front of you is likely to be able to help you or not:

1. **X as in Expertise:** How well does the headhunter know the client, the candidate, the industry or at least the position they represent? This will directly influence the quality of work and career advice delivered. Some recruiters do not even have the basic information—vital puzzle pieces you need to know to take a decision with such an impact on you. Ask these questions to sort the wheat from the chaff: What is the position's history? The reason for the vacancy? Who are the direct competitors of the company they recruit for? What are the current trends the industry is undergoing? How does your headhunter find their candidates? How well can your headhunter describe the desired candidate's personality and the culture of the client?

2. **X as in Experience:** Are you in front of a specialist or a generalist? Even though being a generalist is nothing bad, some sectors like IT or insurance are very specific, and it is not easy to understand how these areas tick. How many years has your executive search consultant been working in this industry, and what exactly did they do? "Recruitment" can mean temp staffing, interim management, or direct search. Every market and every approach is completely different. And by the way, how many candidates have they recruited in their career? The answers to these questions will give you an indication whether you are in front of a real professional or not.

3. **X as in X-Factor:** The first two points are tangible and measurable, but this is not so with point 3: does your headhunter listen to you, give advice? Are they critical? Do they add insights to your perception of the market? Do they keep promises, e.g. ("I'll call you back on Friday"), brief you before meetings, stress positive as well as critical parts of the desired candidate/the job? These are the soft factors, and they will determine whether you keep in touch in the long run or not. Most headhunters are able to make a good first impression, but few can establish a lasting relationship based on trust and with the goal to create a win–win alliance with you.

Use the 3X "them in Expertise, Experience and X-Factor" to recognize a good headhunter, find and test two to three search consultants, keep in touch with them, and talk to them in a way which puts you in the best possible light.

Q: What are the best ways a jobseeker can engage with a recruiter?

Jorg Stegemann: "The saying goes, 'You cannot fax a handshake.' At some point in time, we must meet each other, look into each other's eyes, and speak. Try to get an interview, but even this is not so easy. When you have a first rejection, try other ways: as in all networking, give first, receive second. What can you give a recruiter so they will be grateful and return the favor? Give business leads, forward an article ('Hi, John, I thought of you when reading this'). It is about creating a relationship. And this cannot be done by LinkedIn or by e-mail or even by seeing each other [only] once.

"People tell us we do not follow up. Well, from my experience (I have conducted 2,500 interviews), I can tell you that 95 out of 100 candidates never follow up either. We meet for one hour, we both (try to) make a good impression, and then—nothing. Treat your recruiter as you want to be treated. Do a better follow-up than we do, stay in touch, be sincere and authentic, and we will fight for you!"

- **Prefer a specialist to a generalist:** If you work in banking, find a headhunter who deals with banking people all day long, as they will have a solid understanding of what you are talking about, what the client is looking for and how to counsel you best.

- **Be careful:** Do not give out confidential information about you or your employer on the phone without having met the headhunter or knowing who their customer is. There are some black sheep out there that are collecting résumés without an assignment. Find out how your headhunter works; if they send out résumés without asking you or if they send "candidate flashes," I would personally change the headhunter.

- **Be rare:** Do not work with more than three headhunters. We try not to present a candidate who has already been sent by our competitor. You, on the other hand, will make a desperate impression if this happens.

- **Be prepared:** I see candidates being late for the interview, badly dressed or with an outdated résumé to the interview and then tell me, "You know, this is only because you are the recruiter. I would never do that for the *real* interview." Prepare your interview well, Google us beforehand, meet us on eye level, and you will impress us and motivate us to do all we can for you.

- **Be honest:** Do not lie to us, as we will probably discover the truth through questioning or ref checks. I immediately stop the interview and blacklist the candidate when they are lying to me (usually when it is about the reasons for leaving or the last salary). We can talk about anything, and if there are bumpy parts in your career, we will sort out how to explain them to our customer. But we must know.

- **Like us or leave us:** Sympathy is an easy thing: If you do not like us, this will probably be the same vice versa. I have rarely placed candidates I did not like. We are networkers, salespeople, and if we like you, we will have a more convincing pitch. If you do not trust or like your recruiter, meet a competitor, and ask the first one to delete you from their records.

- **Use us:** A good headhunter will give you feedback on your presentation and your résumé and will brief you thoroughly on the client, including the people you will meet there. We know what the biggest challenges will be, what it takes to succeed in this given company, and why the job is vacant. We met your potential boss long before you did. Maybe we have even met former employees and know the weak parts of this organization. Ask for this information if your headhunter does not give it.

- **Keep in touch:** Even successful headhunters place only 10 percent of the candidates they meet. Maybe you will not get the job you applied for—but you should do everything to make sure you get the next one that comes along. The biggest lie headhunters tell every day is "I will call you next Monday." Nine times out of ten they do not. If we do not call you, be strong and remind us in a gentle yet persistent way every other week: call us, send a message via LinkedIn, another time write an e-mail.

Q: What should jobseekers not do in relation to recruiters?

"Lie (typically about the reasons for leaving and the last salary): we might find out and if we do, you will be blacklisted. We are like doctors tell us the truth, and we will see what we can do."

Conclusion: A good headhunter with good values and business ethics can be far more efficient in your jobsearch than you. His or her job is to find a job for you. Do not forget that we have the same goal: if you get the job, we get the money. Use us wisely, and we can be a catalyst for your career.

Applicant tracking systems and psychological profiling/testing

ECONOMY: The Great Recession of 2008 caused thousands of candidates to flood the jobs market when few openings existed and businesses were reducing every conceivable duplication of effort to decrease both staff and expenses. Here is my personal historical perspective on how technology and psychological profiling have been integrated into the hiring process in an effort to find the best candidates in an ocean of possibilities.

A historical perspective

As I have watched the changes in hiring practices since 2008 and the beginning of the Great Recession, I have made the following observations:

1. The great recession of 2008 flooded the jobs market through a plethora of layoffs. The sheer number of candidates that applied for positions necessitated quick screening of applications. Hiring communities reached out to the technology world for help, and the applicant tracking systems (ATSs) picked up steam to help.

2. The first ATSs were dismal for both jobseekers and employers.

3. As revenues plunged, executive leadership was pressured to turn a profit.

4. Additional layoffs reduced expenses and increased profit margins. This served to appease stockholders as hiring professionals were pressured with "If you hired the right people, we would be making a profit!"

5. Hiring professionals were caught in a no-win situation. The companies were unwilling to pay for top talent. HR needed better tools.

6. Talent management companies mushroomed and promoted the use of psychological profiling to determine the best candidates for a position.

7. Hiring communities bought in—if a new hire didn't work out, they could blame the talent management company and perhaps find a new one. HR was less vulnerable.

8. ATSs continued to improve; at the time of this writing, however, hiring professionals are not convinced that they are finding the best talent.

9. Finding the right hires to build businesses and grow profitability will continue to be a high priority. The pressure on everyone—employees, hiring professionals, and executives—is sometimes crushing. No one wants to be the cause of a business failure.

These observations may not reflect the "spin" applied by talent management and recruiting companies when they promote the use of these assessments. However, I stand by my convictions regarding the content here on their use of psychological testing.

Psychological testing is not the same as a skill or interest inventory. Psychological testing, according to the American Psychological Association, is:

> "similar to medical tests . . . . The results will be used to inform [and] develop a treatment plan.
>
> Psychological evaluations serve the same purpose. Psychologists use tests and other assessment tools to measure and observe a client's behavior to arrive at a diagnosis and guide treatment."
>
> *http://www.apa.org/helpcenter/assessment.aspx*

As a career consultant, strategist, and job coach, I have grave issues, both ethical and professional, with the use of psychological assessments in the hiring process.

I did it myself (Marcia the Guinea Pig)

When my clients began taking these assessments, I contacted a talent management agency and asked if they would put me through their battery of tests and show me how their process could help companies make good hiring decisions.

The tests took about ninety minutes to complete. I really wanted to see if they could help companies make good hiring decisions, so I abandoned any skepticism as I followed the process.

Three weeks later I was debriefed during a two-hour session. I received a 72-page computer-generated report that included comments that were terse, judgmental, and often carrying mixed messages.

One place indicated that I show great "Persistence in job completion." Yet "She may lose interest in a project once the challenge ceases." Huh?

The composite overview was accurate in some areas and not in others. It accurately cited challenges that I experienced, especially early in my career, but did not make any attempt to identify whether I had learned to manage any of the "negative attributes."

My experience with the results leaves the use of the assessment highly suspicious. The candidate responds to questions without context. And it is impossible for assessments to be specific with regard to behavior in a particular work-place when that workplace is not referenced or experienced by the candidate.

If the assessments are inaccurate (mine was in several key areas!), the misconception remains in the minds of the decision makers.

Truly the information in the report could be used equally well to find reason to fire me or hire me—depending on the objective of the person reading it.

Another concern regards the handling of highly personal information. The person I spoke with could not tell me where my information was being kept, for how long, or if there were safeguards to ensure it would not be used inappropriately. He could not define *inappropriate use* of the information. He did not know if the information could be subpoenaed or used in a court of law.

What? Every person who takes these assessments should be asking about the security of this confidential information.

The only encouraging outcome from the meeting was this: The talent management company made it clear that the results of these tests should constitute not more than 12 percent of the hiring decision.

For my client, whose scores weren't "close enough," these tests were a total elimination round.

Critical points about the use of psychological testing

Point 1: I hope it is clear that these tests originated to help people who suffer from psychological illness, hence my ethical issues with their use as a tool for hiring and promotion decisions. I also have ethical issues with repurposing these tests for employment decisions.

Point 2: The information should be protected by the legal system. To date, nothing is in place to protect jobseekers, employees, or employers. Clearly this is a gross oversight.

Pearson's Clinical Assessment and Talent Assessment Group addresses concerns and offers ethical guidelines. Current HIPAA law should be applicable to these practices. *http://www.pearsonclinical.com/legal.html#ethical*

Point 3: These assessments do not bring value to the hiring process. the University of Pennsylvania study *The Use of Personality Tests as a Hiring Tool: Is the Benefit Worth the Cost?* finds that

> there is very little that interferes with an employer's ability to utilize personality tests.

> First, some of the most widely used tests for screening job applicants were not developed for that purpose.

> . . . there is conflicting evidence about the extent to which personality measures are valid predictors of job performance.

> Therefore, making assumptions about what emotional states should be sought is dangerous.

> Even assuming one can successfully identify what personality traits are desired in an employee for a particular position, there are reasons to doubt the ability of many commonly used personality inventories to identify the best candidates for a job.

> This makes their application to the workplace questionable.

Do psychological tests function as a best practice for hiring?
It's a myth!

Hiring entities think they are getting good information for hiring decisions—but it's a myth! In fact, I believe it is a hoax, and it's harmful. It may be fascinating, but it's hurting people and misinforming businesses.

Not all assessments are "psychological," and I have no issue with using nonpsychological testing to help individuals understand their natural inclinations where success may be more likely. However, even these can be misleading. Do you know anyone who struggled with math and then got their degree in (you guessed it) math?

Best practices

Our best work is done with the right balance of challenge and a secure work environment. It's different for every person. I do not believe that we should be using this kind of personal and private information to make hiring or promotion decisions. It belongs to individuals—to help them understand and make decisions for themselves.

If companies want to make good hiring decisions, then they might consider taking the time to get to know their candidates. It would be more cost-effective than these profiles. I also believe that true hiring professionals know how to make a good hire. To do so, they need the financial support for salaries and the time to do their job well.

Here are some comments regarding the use of psychological testing from some talent management websites:

Dr. Janda has worked with companies to perform psychological assessments of potential employees and employees under consideration for promotion. (*cindexinc.com*)

"Harrison assessment accurately measures employee passion for specific jobs . . . automating acquisition, career planning and succession planning." (*http://www.harrisonassessments.com/system-overview-video.html*)

In this one-minute video, a vice president from Korn/Ferry International, a leader in the recruitment industry, uses these assessments to "view . . . the candidates' values, motivations, and emotional intelligence." *https://www.youtube.com/watch?v=KtahCCZywOI&t=56*

Hope: The author wishes to encourage hiring professionals to be protagonists in their hiring entities to identify and find better ways to identify the best candidates. We haven't found them yet.

If psychological tests are to be used in the employment arena, then protection of the information is critical, and hiring professionals should insist on identifying a means to protect jobseekers, employees, and the businesses that use them.

Lastly, as we become a global economy and employees are asked to cross cultural and national borders, clear protections will require international consent. I look to the professional human resource establishments, such as SHRM, to take the national and international lead on these matters.

From the jobseeker's perspective

The Great Recession brought about substantial changes for jobseekers. Many people were stunned at finding themselves jobless and under intense pressure to compete for the few available jobs. The new applicant tracking systems, which were in their infancy, were horrible for both jobseekers and hiring professionals.

Jobseekers were desperate and many went to great lengths to get interviews. They bombarded former colleagues who had managed to keep their jobs. One person told me she was afraid to leave the office building during lunch because former colleagues were waiting to ask for advice, recommendations, and requests to submit their résumés to HR.

Faced with the daunting online systems, the applicant tracking systems (ATSs), jobseekers tried every conceivable idea to get past them, through them, and around them—or in some way find the hiring manager and beg for an opportunity to be considered for whatever position might be available.

Early in the Great Recession, the overriding attitude toward the newly unemployed included an assumption that they were "dead wood." The unemployed were disgraced, embarrassed, and ashamed. It took a full year before the reality set in that the problem was not the employees. Business leaders had made terrible business decisions, companies had become greedy, and to appease the stakeholders and manage profits, millions of people were laid off.

With the market saturation of jobless applicants and the diminishing pool of available jobs, many jobseekers became disheartened. By 2012, the most popular formula to calculate the length of unemployment was one month for every $10,000 of salary in the new job. *http://www.bizjournals.com/washington/ blog/2012/07/how-long-will-your-job-search-take.html*

This formula did not take into consideration the massive changes brought on by technology and the impact of the housing industry's collapse. Some industries simply shut down. Printing came to a halt as mobile devices and online marketing replaced print. Travel accommodations were now made online. Office supplies dwindled as cloud technologies began to eliminate the need for paper copy. As the housing market came to a standstill, concrete products, lumber, and the home furnishing industry shut down.

State and federal programs were thrown together as quickly as possible to help jobseekers reskill and certify.

Jobseekers in declining industries generally tried to find jobs like those they had left. It could take six months to realize that their industry was declining and they needed to transfer their skills or develop new ones. Finding a new career-track, identifying potential programs to reskill and certify, and then completing the program could easily take 18 months. Consequently, unemployment benefits, in some cases, were extended as long as 99 weeks. *http://www.forbes.com/sites/ timworstall/2015/01/31/extended-unemployment-benefits-really-did-raise-the-unemployment-rate-they-still-are/.*

Many jobseekers, frustrated and hopeless, quit their jobsearch. The new vocabulary included *long-term unemployed*, and it continues seven years later at the writing of this book.

Hope: Through these years of disheartened change, government programs were not enough, and most were limited in their scope. To answer the need, many civic organizations mobilized to help the jobseeker. Libraries across the US began researching employment programs and bringing in key speakers for jobseekers and entrepreneurs. They offered space for weekly jobseeker support groups and monthly publications of support opportunities; most important, they restored dignity as jobseekers comprehended the scope of the problem, realized they had done nothing wrong, and joined together to support and establish hope with their jobseeking colleagues. Speakers in the hiring industry donated their time and expertise to support the jobless through résumé writing, interview techniques, and the use of LinkedIn. Finance professionals helped them organize and manage their finances. Lawyers assisted jobseekers at risk of losing their homes.

Many jobseekers decided to start their own businesses. Again, in the US many organizations mobilized, coordinated, and collaborated to offer assistance to start-up businesses. These assistance programs spanned the range from managing the registration of a new business, small business research, and database access through dedicated library personnel, as well as the need for microloans for start-ups and a multitude of SCORE volunteers (Service Corps of Retired Executives) to guide and coach new business owners.

Closing

Perhaps the greatest contribution of the Great Recession has been the revival of Americans helping Americans. As individuals merge into global e-commerce and move from competition to collaboration, and as social assets continue to bring greater value, we will become a workforce where individuals help each other. This will be a part of our career management process.

As we move forward, it is critical for us to think through the enormity of these changes that are now a constant. We will need a flexible set of tools that will allow us all to enjoy a consistent income for as long as we live. That is what Part Two of this book is about.

Marcia: During the year prior to the writing of this book, it has become evident that this highly touted "Generation Me" has very quickly changed their mind-set, their outlook, and their approach to career strategy and their lives in general. They may still be the "me, me, me" generation and—as this article in *USA Today* indicates—believe that "self first" is a good thing. *http://www.usatoday.com/story/money/business/2013/08/24/millenials-time-magazine-generation-y/2678441/* However, I have noticed a change in the expression of this seemingly self-centered approach.

First, millennials do believe that "self first" is good and important. I have noticed that this doesn't necessarily have negative connotations as older generations may be led to believe. The millennials who come through my career practice see what the large corporate business and hiring practices have done to their parents and boomer relatives. They don't want any part of it. (Interestingly, neither do many boomers who come through my practice.)

Further, these individuals are graduating from high school and college with the added weight of the economy, the environment, the depleted Social Security challenges (in the US), and a culture shattered and divided on numerous fronts. They want something better! They want nonviolent ways of resolving differences, and they want to make a difference in the environment and in the lives of people with daily, real-life needs. If this is the expression of the "Me" mind-set, then I believe we should join them, champion them, and promote them. Surely they will find creative solutions that we boomers would never think about or even consider. *http://www.usatoday.com/story/money/business/2013/08/24/ millenials-time-magazine-generation-y/2678441/*

Quick career strategy review

The "strategy" is the process outlined in previous sections to:

1. Identify employment opportunities that fit as defined by:
   a. Your values
   b. Your attributes
   c. Your skills
   d. Your environment
   e. A viable market

2. Create and maintain a toolbox of written information for potential hiring professionals.

3. Clearly articulate your organizational value and Unique Value Statement to a variety of people.

4. Maintain a network of select contacts who will speak on your behalf.

Once these tools are in place, it is time to implement your jobsearch.

Jobsearch implementation process

As with any new process, it is healthy to expect to need to tweak and make changes.

Generally, a person is evaluated through their written documentation. The purpose of these documents is to prompt a person-to-person conversation of some kind. The options are varied and include Skype, a phone call, webcam, FaceTime, virtual meeting room with VoIP (Voice over Internet Protocol) . . . and the list goes on. The point here is that once a jobseeker applies for a position, there should be a positive response.

Application submission and response

My rule of thumb is simple. Jobseekers should receive some kind of response for every five applications they file. If, after a reasonable amount of time (7–10 days), nothing comes back after five submissions, then it is time to review what is being sent. The options are few:

1. The jobseeker is applying for positions that they not qualified for or are otherwise not a good fit.

2. The written application (cover letter and/or résumé) has a problem that has not been adequately managed:
   a. Something needs to be added.
   b. Something needs to be taken off.
   c. Something needs to be fixed.

3. The presentation is problematic in some way (e.g., too small a font).

Potential issues that cause elimination

Hiring professionals see an enormous quantity of applications and subsequently jobseekers. As professionals, they develop an ability to quickly evaluate and ascertain matches between positions and candidates. It is the responsibility of the jobseeker to quickly and clearly educate these professionals so they select the jobseeker to move forward in the hiring process.

Here is a partial checklist of potential reasons that candidates are eliminated:

- The candidate is not qualified for the position (applied for the wrong position).

- The candidate has not convincingly demonstrated their qualifications.

- There are errors in the presentation (e.g., grammar, spelling, poor formatting, errors in dates, company names).

- There is a "sense" that the documentation is deceptive or misleading or contains untruthful information (e.g., inflated results statements or responsibilities).

- There are unmanaged concerns (e.g., gaps in employment, unfinished education, a new job every few years).

Encouraging additional support

When a potential position becomes available that is especially appealing, I encourage jobseekers to engage with their network or intentionally connect with potential associates to gain additional information and possibly promote the jobseeker's application. This doesn't have to be as awkward as it sounds. However, having social connections through LinkedIn or other social platforms is an obvious advantage.

Engaging your network

There are endless ways to engage your network and those you have not met who may be able to help. Several suggestions are listed here as a springboard to possibilities.

1. Identify people in your network who have worked at the target company in the past (or if they know someone who worked there) and ask for 15–30 minutes to discuss the culture and internal processes. Ask if they have any insight into the hiring process and if there is anything specific that can be done to promote your candidacy.

2. Repeat Number 1 with people who currently work at the target company.

3. Identify people through LinkedIn or other means whom you might contact. Again, ask for 15–30 minutes to discuss the culture and gather any of their insights regarding the company. LinkedIn Groups, especially those who are specifically related

to the company, may be helpful in identifying potential contacts.

4. Scour the company website for possible contacts and e-mail addresses that may be utilized.

Important note: Try to find one or two contacts. If the hiring community receives a shower of communiqués, it doesn't necessarily work in your favor. Your tone when contacting and speaking to these individuals should be a genuine inquiry. Respond with a thank-you note. Later, when the process is over, reconnect and briefly let the person know how it worked out. That person went out of their way to help you. That's a good contact and one to be nurtured.

Troubleshooting the jobsearch process

There are two major pet peeves that surface when I'm talking to jobseekers.

Major Pet Peeve No. 1

The first deals with individuals who have been at the jobsearch for over four months. During that time, they have worked on their cover letter and résumé and applied to 20 or 30 employment opportunities. Nothing has happened. They have not received one phone call or inquiry.

Here's my pet peeve: they continue to do the exact same thing, over and over again. Generally, these individuals complain about the unfairness of the hiring processes.

Major Pet Peeve No. 2

My second pet peeve is similar to the first one. In these situations, jobseekers read furiously, attend multiple jobseeker groups, listen to as many speakers as possible, read voraciously across the Internet, and engage with every person who will spend five minutes with them. They make note of every suggestion and immediately implement it.

Here is my pet peeve: There is so much change in their jobsearch efforts that it is impossible to track the changes and find a cause and effect. Generally, these individuals are in a constant state of exhaustion. If and when something positive happens, it is impossible to determine the cause and capitalize on the change for future opportunities.

Steps in the jobsearch:

Every jobsearch progresses through eight to ten steps. Each step has the potential to terminate that particular application. Depending on the severity of the issue, the blunder could also keep a jobseeker from being considered for other positions within a company or other positions that a particular recruiter has on his or her docket.

The graphic shows the troubleshooting steps in the jobsearch process.

Each step should be carefully examined and tracked to identify possible issues and manage them as quickly, efficiently, and early in the jobsearch as possible.

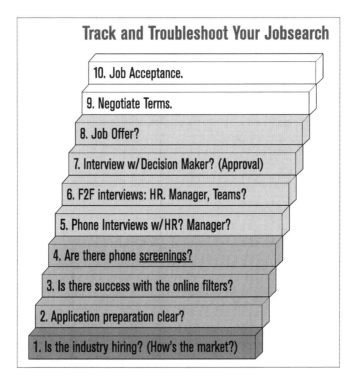

Track and Troubleshoot Your Jobsearch

10. Job Acceptance.

9. Negotiate Terms.

8. Job Offer?

7. Interview w/ Decision Maker? (Approval)

6. F2F interviews: HR. Manager, Teams?

5. Phone Interviews w/ HR? Manager?

4. Are there phone <u>screenings</u>?

3. Is there success with the online filters?

2. Application preparation clear?

1. Is the industry hiring? (How's the market?)

OUTLINE: Troubleshooting the jobsearch process:

1. The jobseeker applies for five positions. Nothing comes back.
   a. The written application (cover letter and/ or résumé) has a problem that has not been adequately managed:
      i. Something needs to be added.
      ii. Something needs to be taken off.
      iii. Something needs to be fixed.
   b. The presentation is problematic in some way (e.g., too small a font).

    c. The jobseeker is applying to positions they are not qualified for.

2. The jobseeker receives a phone call, and then the process stops.
   a. The jobseeker failed to respond appropriately to the caller's concerns.
   b. The jobseeker failed to demonstrate his or her ability to add value (the UVS).
   c. The jobseeker is applying to positions they are not qualified for.

3. The jobseeker receives face-to-face interviews with HR but is not moved forward in the process.
   a. The jobseeker failed to respond appropriately to concerns.
   b. The jobseeker failed to demonstrate his or her ability to add value (the UVS).

4. The jobseeker moves through the entire hiring process but is not offered the position.
   a. Not a concern unless the scenario is repeated three times.
   b. Reference checks, financial checks, or background checks reveal a problem.
   c. Check for nonverbal concerns:
      i. Jobseeker talks too fast, too much energy.
      ii. Doesn't exhibit a high level of interest.
      iii. Some kind of odd behavior (e.g., a facial gesture).

Identifying the place in the process where the problem exists is key to solving the problem. This is where a professional coach may play an important and critical role in troubleshooting. The process can be painful from an emotional standpoint, but it's better to deal with it than prolong the jobsearch.

Case study: Multiple issues:

Nikki is a graduate from a top Ivy League school. She has applied for positions as a research assistant at various companies. After six or seven applications, she had not received any response. Her cover letters and résumés looked good. (Actually, they looked stellar!)

I couldn't find anything objectionable, so I removed all personal information and sent her materials to a few HR colleagues. They all came back within minutes with the same feedback: Nikki had a minor in art history. (So?) I was told to remove it from her résumé. Why? Because Nikki was applying to positions where she would work with high-level executives, and a minor in art history might indicate that her personality was less assertive. She was seen as "weak."

We removed the reference to her art history minor, and Nikki began to receive phone interviews. (Which amazed me!) Over a period of three or four weeks and following four or five phone interviews, Nikki called. She was frustrated that she hadn't been called for any face-to-face interviews.

I asked her to send me her materials for a few positions that she had applied to and hired a colleague to call and interview her. The problem became evident: on the phone,

Nikki sounds flat and uninterested. The truth is that she is intelligent and focused.

Solution: We added one comment to her phone interview wrap-up: *"People tell me that I'm a very focused individual, and I know that I can sound flat over the phone. However, I want you to understand that I believe this is an excellent position for me, and I want to move forward in your process. Is there anything that would prevent you from moving my candidacy forward?"*

That was it. She landed a research job with a top legal firm in Boston.

PART SIX

MANAGING YOUR LONG-TERM STRATEGY (LIFE CYCLE)

Your long-term career strategy should be a repeating cycle that is vibrant and dynamic—it must be flexible and encourage change. In addition, it should maintain your vision for future possibilities with flexible options on how to achieve your goals. One primary goal is maintaining a reliable personal revenue stream.

Career life-cycle management overview

If you followed the process to identify jobs that fit, then you have a carefully crafted, thoughtful foundation. Revisiting your lists of values, attributes, and skills and the optimum environment is an integral part of this process.

As our lives and careers progress, our values may shift. They may change slowly, but noticing the changes and tracking the trends and influences is an essential part of self-awareness.

These personal shifts are a response to changes in our world, both locally and at large. Here is a partial list of influences:

- Our local to global economy (e.g., the closing or opening of a local manufacturing plant).

- Personal financial gains or losses (e.g., an unexpected inheritance or personal loss).

- Health changes to oneself, to a loved one, or locally (e.g., a debilitating disease to yourself or to a parent, or an environmental hazard linked to a community-wide illness).

- An increase or decrease in land values, especially if you own or want to purchase a home.

- An increase or decrease in taxes on any level, from local to national.

For most people, the impact of the national economy has become an integral part of our daily news. This may not be a change for people outside the US; however, the US is so large that the initial impact of our state government frequently receives more attention and has a greater impact on our lives. Interstate commerce brought about an expansion of news coverage, and as the US government grew exponentially, the media helped citizens become informed about the effects on their daily lives.

As social media flourished, individual awareness of global news (within 24 hours, if not sooner) has made its way into the lives of everyone who is technologically connected and wants to know. It is easy to become a news-junkie. Being selective of what to consume can be a challenge, especially as information (syndicated or not) is widely available. No one in a technology-based economy can claim that they don't have access to information or that they are unable to follow national or global trends. Today, these two are integrally linked.

Once again, technology has raised our awareness of the impact of the global economy, which is now a significant factor on individual career management. Change is constant. Every person who wants to remain employed will need to learn to embrace change, manage change, and then strategize change itself to manage risks and threats to their personal income stream.

An example of how this may play out in real life is given following the next section.

Career life-cycle management: Process

This chapter outlines a process to ensure you are managing your long-term career goals and doing everything you can to protect a reliable revenue stream and remain aligned with your ideal employment characteristics as defined earlier in this book.

1. Revisit your values, attributes, skills, and environment

As we respond to these changes, our values, attributes, skills and optimal work environment may change. Here are a few examples:

- If a health challenge affects oneself or someone close, the *value* of available health care options may increase.

- As global communities become the norm, a person may embrace inclusiveness as an *attribute.*

- Skill sets will change dynamically as unused skills fall away and *new skills* are added.

- The *work environment* is ever changing. Virtual engagement and technology engage commerce 24/7. A person may not "go" to work in a physical sense but instead be "at" work for most of their day.

As changes occur in the jobs market and the workplace, some skills will remain and others will fade out. If you want a continuous, dependable revenue stream, then it is your responsibility to track these changes, maintain an awareness of trends, and remain relevant to potential employers.

Review your lists of values, attributes, skills and work environment every six months. If you find that rapid changes have occurred, reschedule your review to every three months, and maintain it until the pace of change slows down.

2. Assess market trends, adapt your expertise, articulate these changes to your network

As our careers progress, we gain knowledge. As we become adept at applying that knowledge in different business contexts, we develop expertise. Having "expertise" in the business community is an essential part of career development.

However, the title *expert* can be a two-edged sword. On the one hand, deeper expertise may be able to demand higher compensation. On the other hand, expertise can be confining. It can be difficult for the expert to break out of the perception that their expertise amounts to the totality of their organizational value. And if a particular expertise is no longer needed, then the individual is perceived as no longer capable of bringing value and may be laid off.

As we move toward a new career model, the jobsearch will be a constant. Periods of employment may actually interrupt the jobsearch. In order to remain employed, each person will need to track those elements that will impact their career trajectory in order to make the best possible decisions to maintain a continuous and consistent income.

Manage and adapt your expertise

Businesses have a short list of activities that generate revenue. It's often called the product life cycle. Every business has a product life cycle, and by tracking its four stages, an employee can forecast whether the product will continue to generate jobs.

However, disruptive innovations can cut a life cycle short. Therefore, it becomes essential to stay current on what is happening within an industry and within a company.

Here are the four stages of the product life cycle:

1. Introduction of the product
2. Growth of the product
3. Maturity of the product
4. Decline of the product

Case study: Adapting skill sets to a changing market

In the example below, Sal (not his real name) watches his industry as well as his customers to

- Manage his career,

- Grow and leverage his network, and

- Ensure a continuous income.

Sal is a business-to-business (B2B) salesperson in the printing industry. Sal contacts businesses and regularly visits with them to clearly understand their challenges. Sal is a consultative salesman—a collaborative partner for his customers, who are primarily business owners.

Initially, Sal helped businesses grow by printing business cards, flyers, promotional postcards, mailers, newsletters, and the like. Graphic design companies were part of his network, and he often recommended them to his customers.

With the advent of e-mail marketing and social media, online marketing took over the advertising market. Sal remembered the day when a customer excitedly mentioned that she had made a sale through an e-mail. Sal followed changes in the industry and watched as best practices developed. By promoting the graphic design companies, he was well known for his collaborative nature and interest in promoting businesses. He had developed a vast integrated business network. As the printing industry began to weaken, he easily secured a new position assisting businesses with the move to online e-commerce.

In Sal's new role, he helped his clients with all their graphic needs for websites, social media, e-mail marketing, and platforms like Facebook and Pinterist. He went out of his way to find companies that could bring video marketing to his customers to complement their online sales promotions. With the need for talented writers to write website copy, create blogs, and produce e-books, Sal identified certified content writers and began referring them to costumers who were struggling.

New inventions and technologies began flooding the market. When 3D printing started to become popular, Sal watched the market and began making connections with printing companies that were leaders in the application of the new technology. Big Data companies were starting to advertise to small businesses. That was Sal's cue to shift his focus, add to his collaborative business network, and continue to bring an additional layer of business value to his customers.

Company-specific product life cycle management

Many companies have a culture of product adoption that brings in new products, "center-stages" them, and sunsets them before the normal market decline begins. The hope is that the next product is ahead of the competition. Other companies may focus on the "low-hanging fruit" in the secondary markets, which may follow the early adopters. The point is that every jobseeker should spend the time to understand the product life cycle of their company and monitor their job stability accordingly.

 Ask the following questions every quarter if your line of business is going through intense change. If it has just come through a change cycle, then consider these questions every six months.

If you are currently employed:

- ❏ What are the products that generate revenue where I work?

- ❏ What phase of the product life cycle are they in?

- ❏ What innovations are coming to market that could impact the life cycle?

- ❏ Is my company aware of them, and are they making plans to manage change?

- ❏ Who are the key players (people and companies) in the innovations?

- ❏ How can I connect with experts in the new areas?

- ❏ What can I bring to these new network assets?

General considerations

Having connections within a company is a critical step in ensuring your future. If a company is not making plans to sunset a product and build revenue in other ways, then you need to watch carefully. If the product you are involved with is moving into the decline stage, then moving to a different area of the company may be in your best interest.

Everyone should intentionally network and build relationships with people in the IT function of their business. Networking with technology specialists in other companies takes on special importance if their current company does not have an IT department. Many smaller companies outsource their IT services. These IT service companies have a broader view of the business and industry landscape. Periodic conversations with account managers and IT service providers can bring insight into current industry trends.

Considerations: Is a merger or acquisition being planned?

The long-range focus on data intelligence mandates that every company collects data. Consequently, every M&A brings a conversion of databases. So when any part of the IT community gets involved in a data convergence, it's your cue to investigate the possibility that a merger or acquisition may be on the horizon.

My suggestion is to create a network of individuals from different business units throughout the company. Touching base with these contacts to discuss key initiatives and changes in them can give you an awareness of potential changes.

Here are a few thoughts on what to look for that might signal an M&A:

Potential external considerations:

- Changes within the industry
- Product changes—dramatic cost changes, shortages, overstock

- Changes in the key technologies that serve the industry
- Market shifts
- Closing of smaller competitors
- Other M&As in the industry

Potential internal indicators:

- Changes in key initiatives
- Projects put on hold or abandoned (especially product launches)
- Employees in HR, accounting, IT, or operations are taken off projects or are unavailable
- Announcement of a new partnership with a consulting company
- Unannounced appearance of consultants
- Unusual requests for information
- Multiple job postings for system analysts
- Rumors . . . which may be true
- Fewer PR announcements about the company

This does not mean that you should brush up your résumé and "jump ship"! Every M&A brings potential opportunity. This emphasizes the importance of being flexible. Any experience you have working across the business or enterprise with different business units (sales, IT, training, HR, product development, etc.) and having weathered an M&A can raise interest for a future employer or recruiter. Your role during the M&A should be clearly demonstrated on your résumé.

Reminder: Hearing about rumors may be helpful and unavoidable; however, encouraging or passing them along is unprofessional. Never speak negatively about an individual, a program, or a company. You never know when such a comment will negatively impact your future.

How do I track change?

At the time of writing, four primary factors must be taken into consideration when tracking change with regard to career paths:

1. Demographics
2. Speed of change
3. Industry change—which is usually brought on by advancements in or applications of technology and globalization
4. Technology

Case study: Demographics

A highly talented musician in Connecticut wanted to teach music. By the time she graduated and passed the exams to become a certified teacher, the demographics of school-age children had changed to the point that schools were shutting down each year. Funding comes from headcount, and the children in school are the offspring of Generation X, which is relatively small. Also impacting the headcount of school-aged children is that the leading edge of Generation Y are waiting five years longer to have children.

Between both of these demographic implications, many school systems will be laying off teachers for several years to come. In many states, the rules are based on union agreements with regard to tenure, so the last teachers to be hired will be the first teachers to be laid off. So this person may get hired but will likely be laid off every spring and find herself competing for a new position every year—at least for several years. There will likely be years where she is hired as a paraprofessional in the schools and earns the minimum hourly wage, working 30 hours per week.

Case study: Speed of change

On my continuous trek to understand and help my clients prepare for their future, the "speed of change" continues to bring astounding revelations with regard to long-term career planning.

One example is a client who went to college to study English and writing so he could become a reporter. But after four years of college, newspapers were shutting down, and social media brought crowd-based information gathering for the now-online newspapers. Reporters were on their way out. The industry looked for independent contributors who had already established themselves as credible writers through the newly established blog platforms. So during the time it took for my client to become credentialed in his career, the career track in his chosen industry had disappeared.

Case study: Industry changes

Another prevalent trend regards changes to the general nature of industries. In other words, what early career jobseekers thought they were going to be doing is no longer the reality. One example is a lawyer who wanted to help the underserved population. She quickly learned that the key drivers in the law firm focus on billable hours. Spending time to understand a potential client that can't be billed by the law firm is clearly monitored by imposed quotas for billable hours each week. Essentially, the job is a sweatshop environment.

Just getting a job can no longer be the goal. The speed of change is mandating that businesses and companies must be flexible and able to adapt quickly if they are going to survive. Many businesses and industries now focus solely on how to build revenue. As the needs of companies change, so will the opportunities, skills, and core competencies that form the foundation of job opportunities. Consequently, some positions will disappear, and others will be generated.

With the speed of change rapidly accelerating, many companies no longer have time or resources to grow talent pools internally. This is especially true in the technology realm. As new technologies are adapted, old technologies are no longer needed and are even abandoned. There is no time to train current employees in a new technology, so new IT professionals are hired, to replace those employees who worked with the old technologies, now laid off. In some companies the entire

IT staff are outsourced, and IT staffing companies provide whatever support is needed. They primarily hire contracted IT specialists and generally pay them an hourly wage, without benefits. Other companies may hire IT specialists for specific projects as contractors. Again they are generally paid an hourly wage without benefits.

Tracking trends in technology

My favorite Internet searches focus on new technologies, disruptions, energy, and the interconnectivity between them. Keeping up with new possibilities and trends is not difficult. Here are a few of my favorite Internet searches and a few titles that surfaced:

- New technology trends that will change the future
  - Five tech trends that will change the mobile world
  - Tech trends that will change the future
  - A guide to the technology trends that are shaping our future
  - The tech trends that will change the world

- New technology in the next five years
  - 10 ways the next 10 years are going to be mind-blowing
  - 23 incredible new technologies you'll see by 2012
  - This will be the most disruptive technology over the next 5 years
  - The world in 2025: 8 predictions for the next 10 years

- Future workplace trends
  - Future workforce trends & challenges
  - The corporate crystal ball: Future workplace trends
  - The future at work
  - Workplace trends in technology, office layout & culture

- Top industry trends _____
  - Business idea trends news & topics
  - The 10 fastest-growing small businesses
  - 5 manufacturing trends that will shape the marketplace

  Note: add a specific industry name to this search for better definition.

- Top energy trends
  - America's power plan: The top 5 trends in the US
  - Top 10 clean energy trends driving the global clean energy revolution
  - Top regulatory trends in energy
  - Top trends defining global shift to clean and renewable energy
  - Energy trends up to 2050—European Commission

- Disruptive technology
  - Disruptive technologies: Advances that will transform life

○ The 10 most disruptive technology combinations

○ The disruption machine

○ Surviving disruption

Top list of life-changers to watch (some with commentaries)

• 3D Printing Even within a year of this writing, 3D printing has launched an entirely new way of thinking. This thinking has proliferated into new industries, and the shortlist mentioned here is only the start. The industry has grown quickly from an intriguing idea to the point that most public libraries now have some kind of 3D printer.

• Renewable energy

• Smart technologies

• Collaborative technology: technology integration such as smart homes, smart cars, and smart (AI) robotics. At the time of this writing social media is being used for marketing as well as crowdsourcing, crowdfunding etc.—it's a group knowledge.

• Robotics, AI

• Nanotechnology

• Biotechnology, pharmacogenetics

PART SEVEN

THE MOST COMPELLING STORY I'VE EVER KNOWN

One of the most compelling stories I've heard is about a young musician that was highly successful as she graduated high school. She had managed and conducted a 60-voice youth choir and earned a full scholarship for her undergraduate school. She graduated with honors as an undergraduate, went to one of the top conservatories, and studied with world-renowned musicians from the Chicago Symphony. After seven years, as one of the first women in the country to hold the position of director of bands at a state university, she returned to school and earned a PhD in adult music education with a cognate in orchestral conducting.

Her early career included both state and private schools. Conducting was her first love. After a summer of study at an international conducting symposium, she won a position as a professional orchestral conductor in Colorado. After four years in that position, she returned to the conservatory to earn an artist diploma in orchestral conducting, earning the top award as outstanding orchestral conductor.

Following graduation, she had to earn a living while she applied to orchestral positions, a process that can take from two to five years. As she thought about her work as a conductor, she applied for a position as a quality assurance consultant in an insurance software company. It was similar to orchestra rehearsal: find the mistakes (computer bugs) and report them to the professional (software programmer). She was sure that she would land a job as a conductor within a year.

After a year, she decided to look for a better position and landed a job as a corporate trainer. After all, isn't corporate training the same as orchestra rehearsal . . . getting everyone on board to do their job together? She found the resources to go overseas and participate in an international orchestra festival. She came home with top honors. She wasn't worried when the company outsourced her division and she was laid off. That was okay; surely, with those top honors, an orchestra job would come through soon.

While she was looking for another job, the horror of September 11, 2001, swept the nation and the world. Finding a job became much more difficult as companies in the insurance world were reeling from the event.

The companies that supported the arts, especially in the reinsurance industry, collapsed. Support for the arts evaporated. At this point, she realized that she would have to admit defeat. It was unlikely that she would ever get back to orchestral conducting.

She returned to her former paradigm of comparing her first love and extracting parts of it that could be repurposed to earn a living. She noticed a huge market for project managers and read a book about it. She realized that every concert was a project: it had a start date and an end date. The project manager's triangle fit perfectly: scope, a time, resources. With the help of top professional career coaches, she rewrote her résumé, transforming her skills and experience as a conductor into those of a project manager. After two months of extensive interviews, she won a position with a Fortune 50 company as a project manager in charge of the training rollout of a new project management methodology. Her salary went into six-digits.

When that project was brought in on time and under budget, she was moved to the human resources division and served in various capacities. She tested new technologies, engaged teams in effective communication workshops, and learned enough programming to create training websites for overseas teams.

When the company decided on a complete corporate makeover, most of her division was laid off. At this point she had held five careers:

1. University professor
2. Orchestral conductor
3. Quality assurance consultant
4. Corporate trainer
5. Project manager and learning technologist

What to do next? Her work in the corporate setting, helping teams with communication initiatives, had been highly successful. She seemed to have a knack for helping people find their ideal place in the organization. As she wondered what she should do next, she thought about what her careers had in common. Ideas began to take shape.

As a university professor, she helped college seniors land their first jobs as music teachers. Her work as an orchestral conductor was all about communication and helping people work well together. In the quality assurance business, she mastered finding errors and delivering the bad news to the programmers. As a corporate trainer and project manager, she was helping people become more effective in the workplace through better communication.

She had spent hours listening to the frustrations of people who didn't like their jobs and who thought they were stuck in their career track. Some research showed five out of six grads lost their first job in the first three to six months. Now why was that? Because the job wasn't a good fit!

That realization tipped the scale. She launched a company called Grads Forward. She made trips to the two- and four-year schools and found significant interest in bringing in a program to help grads find jobs and offer reporting metrics that schools could use in their marketing materials.

It took over a year to develop the first offering. During that time, the Great Recession of 2008 hit. Thousands and thousands of people were laid off. It soon became evident that the available workforce demographic was changing by the day. Companies were hiring the least expensive talent they could, and for a while, early career jobseekers were not having trouble finding work. Meanwhile, mid-career jobseekers were screaming for help as new technologies were used to filter applicants.

She realized that her business model and her offerings had to shift to accommodate the changing demographics. She changed the name of the company to Forward Motion and expanded the offerings to help jobseekers from early career to executives. After six years, the product line was again expanded to offer assistance to small companies to find employees who were a good fit.

Forward Motion is the sixth career. At the writing of this book, it is now in its tenth year. She is now working with millennial jobseekers to clearly understand their challenges and identify solutions for them and for their employers.

I'm sure you've figured out that this is my career biography. I have had six careers, and as the company continues to grow and thrive, the plan and hope is to sell it and become executive director and CEO of TheMasterWorks.org, a nonprofit dedicated to the restoration of community and semiprofessional orchestras throughout the United States.

As for the contents of this book: I rest my case.

GLOSSARY

3D printing—a process for making a physical object from a three-dimensional digital model, typically by laying down many successive thin layers of a material.

401(k) Plan—a defined contribution plan where employees can make contributions from their paycheck (either before or after-tax, depending on the options offered in the plan). The contributions go into a 401(k) account, with the employee often choosing the investments based on options provided under the plan.

Affordable Care Act (ACA), generally referred to as Obamacare—the landmark health reform legislation passed by the 111th Congress and signed into law by President Barack Obama.

AI—Artificial intelligence

Algorithms—a set of steps that are followed in order to solve a mathematical problem or to complete a computer process.

Android—an open-source operating system used for smartphones and tablet computers.

Apple's iOS—iOS (originally iPhone OS) is a mobile operating system created and developed by Apple Inc. and distributed exclusively for Apple hardware. It is the operating system that presently powers many of the company's mobile devices, including the iPhone, iPad, and iPod touch.

Applicant tracking system (ATS)—a software application that enables the electronic handling of recruitment needs. An ATS can be implemented or accessed online on an enterprise or small business level, depending on the needs of the company. Free, open-source ATS software is also available.

Assets—property owned by a person or company, regarded as having value and available to meet debts, commitments, or legacies.

Associated Press (AP)—an American multinational nonprofit news agency headquartered in New York City and operated as a cooperative, unincorporated association.

Baby Boomer—a person born in the years following World War II (1946–1964), when there was a temporary marked increase in the birth rate.

Bank of England—the Bank of England (BoE) is the central bank for the United Kingdom. It has a wide range of responsibilities, similar to those of most central banks around the world. It acts as the government's bank and the lender of last resort. It issues currency and oversees monetary policy.

Basel Accords—agreements set forth by the Basel Committee on Banking Supervision (BCBS), which provides recommendations on banking regulations in regard to capital risk, market risk, and operational risk.

Basel Committee on Banking Supervision (BCBS)—a committee of banking supervisory authorities established in 1975 by the central bank governors of the Group of Ten countries. It provides a forum for regular cooperation on banking supervisory matters.

Black economy—the segment of a country's economic activity that is derived from sources that fall outside of the country's rules and regulations regarding commerce. The activities can be either legal or illegal depending on what goods and/or services are involved.

Bond—a financial instrument of indebtedness of the bond issuer to the holders. It is a debt security, under which the issuer owes the holders a debt and, depending on the terms of the bond, is obliged to pay them interest (the coupon) and/or to repay the principal at a later date, termed the maturity date.

Bond-bingeing—the practice of a government to issue excessively large numbers of government bonds to increase liquidity in the economy and acquire additional revenues to enable government expenditure. (Author's definition.)

C-suite—a widely used slang term collectively referring to a corporation's most important senior executives. C-Suite gets its name because top senior executives' titles tend to start with the letter *C*, for *chief*, as in chief executive officer, chief operating officer, and chief information officer

Capital—wealth in the form of money or other assets owned by a person or organization or available or contributed for a particular purpose such as starting a company or investing.

Captchas—a program or system intended to distinguish human from machine input, typically as a way of thwarting spam and automated extraction of data from websites.

CBS—(an initialism of the network's former name, the Columbia Broadcasting System) an American commercial broadcast television network that is a flagship property of CBS Corporation.

Central bank—a national bank that provides financial and banking services for its country's government and commercial banking system, as well as implementing the government's monetary policy and issuing currency.

Contingency recruiters—high-end executive search firms getting a retainer (up-front fee) to perform a specific search for a corporate officer or other senior executive position. Typically, retained searches tend to be for positions that pay upwards of US$150,000 and often far more.

Council on Foreign Relations (CFR)—a 4900-member United States nonprofit organization, publisher, and think tank specializing in US foreign policy and international affairs. Founded in 1921, it is headquartered in New York City, with an additional office in Washington DC.

Disruptive business models—innovations that create a new market and value network and eventually disrupt an existing market and value network, displacing established market leading firms, products, and alliances. The term was defined and phenomenon analyzed by Clayton M. Christensen beginning in 1995.

e-commerce—commercial transactions conducted electronically on the Internet.

Economic Policy Institute (EPI)—a nonprofit, nonpartisan think tank created in 1986 to include the needs of low- and middle-income workers in economic policy discussions. EPI believes every working person deserves a good job with fair pay, affordable health care, and retirement security.

Equity—the value of the shares issued by a company. Also, the residual value of an asset less the debts attached to it.

European Union (EU)—a political union to which the member states of the EEC are evolving. Based on the Maastricht Treaty, it envisions the eventual establishment of common economic, foreign, security, and justice policies.

European Central Bank (ECB)—the central bank for the euro, it administers monetary policy of the Eurozone, which consists of 19 EU member states and is one of the largest currency areas in the world.

Federal Reserve—the central bank of the United States, also known as the Federal Reserve Bank or simply "the Fed." It was created by the Congress to provide the nation with a safer, more flexible, and more stable monetary and financial system.

Fractional reserve banking—the practice whereby a bank accepts deposits, makes loans or investments, and holds reserves that are equivalent to a fraction of its deposit liabilities. Reserves are held at the bank as currency or as deposits in the bank's accounts at the central bank.

Free market economy—economic system in which prices for goods and services are set freely by the forces of supply and demand and are allowed to reach their point of equilibrium without intervention by government policy. It typically entails support for highly competitive markets and private ownership of productive enterprises.

G-20—an informal group of 19 countries and the European Union, with representatives of the International Monetary Fund and the World Bank. The finance ministers and central bank governors began meeting in 1999, at the suggestion of the G7 finance ministers in response to the global financial crisis of 1997–99.

Generation X—the generation born after that of the baby boomers (roughly from the early 1960s to mid 1970s), often perceived to be disaffected and directionless.

Generation Y—the generation born in the 1980s and 1990s, comprising primarily the children of the baby boomers and typically perceived as increasingly familiar with digital and electronic technology.

Great Recession—a label used by journalists and economists to describe a severe, prolonged economic downturn. Some economists trace the most recent great recession to the collapse of the United States housing market in 2007.

Gross Domestic Product (GDP)—the total value of goods produced and services provided in a country during one year.

H-1B visa—a non-immigrant visa that allows US companies to employ foreign workers in specialty occupations that require theoretical or technical expertise in specialized fields such as architecture, engineering, mathematics, science, and medicine.

Housing bubble—a run-up in housing prices fueled by demand, speculation and the belief that recent history is an infallible forecast of the future.

Human capital—the skills, knowledge, and experience possessed by an individual or population, viewed in terms of their value or cost to an organization or country.

Inflation—a general increase in prices and fall in the purchasing value of money.

Instruments—Financial instruments are tradable assets of any kind. They can be cash, evidence of an ownership interest in an entity, or a contractual right to receive or deliver cash or another financial instrument.

International Labour Organization (ILO)—a United Nations agency dealing with labor issues, particularly international labor standards, social protection, and work opportunities for all.

International Monetary Fund—an international organization, head-quartered in Washington DC, of 189 countries working to foster global monetary cooperation, secure financial stability, facilitate international trade, promote high employment and sustainable economic growth, and reduce poverty around the world.

Internet disintermediation—in finance, the withdrawal of funds from intermediary financial institutions, such as banks and savings and loan associations, to invest them directly. Generally, disintermediation is the process of removing the middleman or intermediary from future transactions.

Jobs Cross-Cutting Solutions Area (CCSA)—a management unit within the World Bank that includes climate change, fragility, conflict and violence, gender, jobs, and public-private partnerships.

Lehman Brothers—a firm once considered one of the major players in the global banking and financial services industries which declared bankruptcy on September 15, 2008, after a catastrophic collapse caused by a mix of subprime mortgage exposure as well as negative rumors and alleged short selling in the market.

Liabilities—Under international financial reporting standards, a financial liability can be either of these two items: A contractual obligation to deliver cash or similar to another entity or a potentially unfavorable exchange of financial assets or liabilities with another entity.

Lump-sum—a single payment made at a particular time, as opposed to a number of smaller payments or installments.

Marginal costs—the cost added by producing one extra item of a product.

Market share—the portion of a market controlled by a particular company or product.

Millennial generation—The term Millennials generally refers to the generation of people born between the early 1980s and the early 2000s. Perhaps the most commonly used birth range for this group is 1982–2000

Mintel—Mintel is the world's leading market intelligence agency. Website. *http://www.mintel.com.* Mintel Group Ltd is a privately owned, London-based market research firm. The corporation also maintains offices in Chicago, New York, Mumbai, Belfast, Shanghai, Tokyo and Sydney.

Money supply—the total amount of money in circulation or in existence in a country.

Moore's Law—an observation made by Intel co-founder Gordon Moore in 1965. He noticed that the number of transistors per square inch on integrated circuits had doubled every year since their invention.

National Center for Health Statistics—The National Center for Health Statistics (NCHS) is a principal agency of the U.S. Federal Statistical System which provides statistical information to guide actions and policies to improve the health of the American people.

National debt—the total amount of money that a country's government has borrowed, by various means.

National Science Foundation—The National Science Foundation (NSF) is an independent Federal agency created by the National Science Foundation Act of 1950, as amended (42 USC 1861–75).

NORC—A naturally occurring retirement community, or NORC (rhymes with "fork"), is a term used to describe a community that has a large proportion of residents over 60 but was not specifically designed to meet the needs of seniors living independently in their homes.

Obamacare—(the Affordable Care Act) is a US healthcare reform law that expands and improves access to care and curbs spending through regulations and taxes.

Offshore accounting—a term used to describe foreign banks, corporations, investments and deposits. A company may legitimately move offshore for the purpose of tax avoidance or to enjoy relaxed regulations. Offshore financial institutions can also be used for illicit purposes such as money laundering and tax evasion.

Organisation for Economic Co-operation and Development (OECD)—The Organisation for Economic Co-operation and Development (OECD) (French: Organisation de coopération et de développement économiques, OCDE) is an intergovernmental economic organisation with 35 member countries, founded in 1961 to stimulate economic progress and world trade.

Pattern recognition—a branch of machine learning that focuses on the recognition of patterns and regularities in data, although it is in some cases considered to be nearly synonymous with machine learning.

Post-industrial age—A post-industrial society is a stage in a society's development during which the economy transitions from one that primarily provides goods to one that primarily provides services.

Productivity—the effectiveness of productive effort, especially in industry, as measured in terms of the rate of output per unit of input.

Profit margins—the amount by which revenue from sales exceeds costs in a business.

Quantitative Easing (QE)—an unconventional monetary policy in which a central bank purchases government securities or other securities from the market in order to lower interest rates and increase the money supply.

Real household income—a measure of the combined incomes of all people sharing a particular household or place of residence. It includes every form of income, e.g., salaries and wages, retirement income, near cash government transfers like food stamps, and investment gains.

Retained search—Also known as Executive search (informally headhunting) is a specialized recruitment service used to source candidates for senior, executive or other highly specialized positions in organizations.

Revenue—the amount of money that a company actually receives during a specific period, including discounts and deductions for returned merchandise.

Silent Generation—the demographic group of people born from the mid 1920s to the early 1940s. The name was originally applied to people in the United States and Canada but has been applied as well to those in Western Europe, Australia and South America. It includes most of those who fought during the Korean War.

Smart technologies—(Self-Monitoring, Analysis and Reporting Technology; often written as SMART) is a monitoring system included in computer hard disk drives (HDDs) and solid-state drives (SSDs) that detects and reports on various indicators of drive reliability, with the intent of enabling the anticipation of hardware failures.

STEM jobs—an acronym for the fields of science, technology, engineering and math. Discussion of STEM-related programs has become a presidential priority because too few college students are pursuing degrees in these fields.

Taulbee survey—The Taulbee Survey is the principal source of information on the enrollment, production, and employment of Ph.D.s in computer science and computer engineering (CS & CE) and in providing salary and demographic data for faculty in CS & CE in North America.

U.S. Bureau of Labor Statistics (BLS)—a unit of the United States Department of Labor. It is the principal fact-finding agency for the U.S. government in the broad field of labor economics and statistics and serves as a principal agency of the U.S. Federal Statistical System.

World Bank Group (WBG)—a family of five international organizations that make leveraged loans to developing countries. It is the largest and most famous development bank in the world and is an observer at the United Nations Development Group.

REFERENCE LIST

AFP Agence France-Presse (2014). World Bank warns of global jobs crisis. Retrieved from: *https://www.yahoo.com/news/world-bank-warns-global-jobs-crisis-050827124.html?ref=gs*

American Management Association AMA Critical Skills Survey (2010). Retrieved from: *http://www.amanet.org/news/AMA-2010-critical-skills-survey.aspx*

Associated Press (2013) NORC Center for Public Affairs Research at the University of Chicago (2013). Working Longer: Older Americans' Attitudes on Work and Retirement.

Bray, Paula (2014). Mr. President, This Is My America: Life in an RV Park With a Master's Degree. *huffingtonpost.com.*

Brynjolfsson, Erik and McAfee, Andrew (2014). The Second Machine Age. *http://secondmachineage.com/*

Chowdhury, A., and Islam, I. (n.d.) Is there an optimal debt-to-GDP ratio? Retrieved from: *http://voxeu.org/debates/commentaries/there-optimal-debt-gdp-ratio*

Christensen, Clayton, interviewed by Suster, Mark (3 March 2013). In 15 Years From Now Half of US Universities May Be in Bankruptcy. Retrieved from: *https://bothsidesofthe table.com/in-15-years-from-now-half-of-us-universities-may-be-in-bankruptcy-my-surprise-discussion-with-979f93bd6874#.mxelnn4hg*

Clifton, Jim (2011). The Coming Jobs War. New York NY: Gallup Press. Retrieved from: *http://www.gallup.com/business journal/156719/ten-demands-america-master.aspx*

Collins, Mike (2015). The Big Bank Bailout. Retrieved from: *http://www.forbes.com/sites/mikecollins/2015/07/14/the-big-bank-bailout/#2d37f9893723*

Duhigg, Charles, and Bradsher, Keith (Jan. 21 2012). The New York Times: How the U.S. Lost out on iPhone Work. Retrieved from: *http://www.nytimes.com/2012/01/22/business/apple-america-and-a-squeezed-middle-class.html?_r=0*

The Economic Collapse Blog (n.d.). 10 Stories From The Cold, Hard Streets Of America That Will Break Your Heart. Retrieved from: *http://theeconomiccollapseblog.com/archives/tag/heartbreaking-stories*

Federal Reserve Bank of San Francisco (January 2013). Community Development Project. Vantage Point.

Frank, Robert (19 September 2013). CNBC. Druckenmiller: Fed robbing poor to pay rich. Retrieved from: *http://www .cnbc.com/2013/09/19/druckenmiller-fed-shifting-money-to-rich-from-poor.html*

FRED Economic Research (n.d.).This chart is retrieved as a composite from the charting tool combining the charts: 1) Real Gross Domestic Product (GDPC1) and 2) Federal Debt: Total Public Debt as Percent of Gross Domestic Product (GFDEGDQ1885); Retrieved from: *https://fred .stlouisfed.org*

Frey, C.B., and Osborne, M.A (2013). The Future of Employment: How Susceptible are Jobs to Computerisation? *http://www.oxfordmartin.ox.ac.uk/downloads/academic/ The_Future_of_Employment.pdf*

G20 Labour and Employment Ministerial Meeting (LEMM) (2014). G20 labour markets: outlook, key challenges and policy responses. Retrieved from: *http://www.ilo.org/global/ about-the-ilo/how-the-ilo-works/multilateral-system/g20/ reports/WCMS_305421/lang--en/index.htm*

Gattuso, James L., and Katz, Diane (13 March 2012). Red Tape Rising: Obama-Era Regulation at the Three-Year Mark.

Gronbach, Ken W. (2008). The Age Curve: How to Profit from the Coming Demographic Storm. American Management Association.

https://books.google.co.uk/books/about/The_Age_Curve.html?
*id=rNAG_9IQ4loC&printsec=frontcover&source=kp_read_*
button&hl=en&redir_esc=y#v=onepage&q&f=false

http://bonoboathome.blogspot.com/2007/01/us-labour-market
.html

Huszar, Andrew (11 November 2013). Confessions of a
Quantitative Easer. The Wall Street Journal Retrieved
from: *http://www.wsj.com/articles/SB1000142405270230*
3763804579183680751473884

International Labour Organization (2015). World Employment
and Social Outlook—Trends 2015. Formerly entitled *Global
Employment Trends.* Retrieved from: *http://www.ilo.org/*
global/research/global-reports/weso/2015/lang--en/index.htm

Iyengar, Rishi (2014). A Global Jobs Crisis Is Coming, Says
World Bank. Retrieved from: *http://time.com/3308095/*
a-global-jobs-crisis-is-coming-says-world-bank/

Manpower Group Talent Shortage Survey Research Results
(2012). Retrieved from: *http://www.manpowergroup.com/wps/*
wcm/connect/6f7772f1-cfe9-4ddd-a573-9a096e8f0e5f/
2012_Talent_Shortage_Survey_Res_US_FINAL_(2).pdf?
MOD=AJPERES

Mischel, Lawrence (29 August 2012). Unions, inequality, and
faltering middle-class wages. Economic Policy Institute.
Issue Brief #342. Retrieved from: *http://www.epi.org/*
publication/ib342-unions-inequality-faltering-middle-class/

The National Academies 21st Century Skill Research (2016). Retrieved from: *https://prezi.com/_klmp2x12957/21st-century-skill-research/*

The National Association of Manufacturers Skills Gap Report (2005). Retrieved from: *http://www.manufacturing.net/article/2011/03/americas-skilled-worker-shortage*

National Science Foundation (2012–2022).

Nelson, Libby (24 June 24 2014). One of the worst for-profit college chains is about to go out of business. Retrieved from: *http://www.vox.com/2014/6/24/5835884/one-of-the-worst-for-profit-college-chains-is-about-to-go-out-of*

Patton, Mike (24 April 2014). Forbes. National Debt Tops $18 Trillion: Guess How Much You Owe?

Pettinger, Tejvan (29 January 2013). Economics Help Blog: Total UK Debt. Retrieved from *http://www.economicshelp.org/blog/4060/economics/total-uk-debt/*

Plumer, Brad (28 February 2013). How the recession turned middle-class jobs into low-wage jobs. The Washington Post.

Rich, Motoko (1 July 2010). Factory Jobs Return, but Employers Find Skills Shortage. Retrieved from New York Times: *http://www.nytimes.com/2010/07/02/business/economy/02manufacturing.html*

Rifkin, Jeremy (2011). The Third Industrial Revolution. *http://www.thethirdindustrialrevolution.com/*

Rifkin, Jeremy (2014). The Zero Marginal Cost Society. *http://www.thezeromarginalcostsociety.com/*

Sedensky, Matt (2013). Associated Press–NORC Center for Public Affairs Research at the University of Chicago. Poll: Half of older workers delay retirement plans. Retrieved from: *http://www.apnorc.org/news-media/Pages/News+Media/poll-half-of-older-workers-delay-retirement-plans.aspx*

Stewart, Heather (13 August 2011). The Guardian. Quantitative easing 'is good for the rich, bad for the poor'. Retrieved from: *https://www.theguardian.com/business/2011/aug/14/quantitative-easing-riots*

Suster, Mark (2013). Both Sides of the Table. Interview: "In 15 years from now half of US universities may be in bankruptcy" Clay Christensen.

The Taulbee Survey (n.d.). Retrieved from: *http://cra.org/resources/taulbee-survey/*

Treanor, Jill (19 January 2016). The Guardian: Fourth industrial revolution set to benefit richest, UBS report says. Retrieved from: *https://www.theguardian.com/business/2016/jan/19/fourth-industrial-revolution-set-to-benefit-richest-ubs-report-says*

Union Bank of Switzerland (UBS) (2016). "Extreme automation and connectivity: The global, regional, and investment implications of the Fourth Industrial Revolution" *https://www.ubs.com/global/en/about_ubs/follow_ubs/highlights/davos-2016.html*

U.S. Bureau of Labor Statistics Employment Projections 2014–24 *http://www.bls.gov/news.release/pdf/ecopro.pdf*

U.S. Bureau of Labor Statistics Occupational Employment and Wage Estimates, May 2011; US Department of Health and Human Services Poverty Guidelines, 2011; American Community Survey 5 Year Estimates, 2011.

Walker, Dinah (August 2013). Council on Foreign Relations Quarterly Update: The U.S. Economic Recovery in Historical Context. Retrieved from: *http://www.cfr.org/united-states/quarterly-update-us-economic-recovery-historical-context/p25774*

INDEX

52320479R00170

Made in the USA
Middletown, DE
18 November 2017